This yearbook belongs to...

....

Esme x

Join me, Joey, Casper, Mickey and Duke in my 2022 yearbook!

This Esme

YEARBOOK

Published by DJ Murphy (Publishers) Ltd, Olive Studio, Grange Road, Farnham, Surrey GU10 2DQ

WHO DID WHAT IN THIS ESME YEARBOOK 2022
Esme Higgs
Contributors Hollie Bladen, Kiera Boyle, Megan Hurley, Bethany Searby, and Hollie's mum
Head of Art and Design Sarah Garland
Designer Lizzi Porter
Lifestyle photographers Lucy Merrell, David Higgs, World Horse Welfare
Managing Director Zoe Cannon
Commercial Director Abi Cannon

This Esme Yearbook is produced under license by DJ Murphy (Publishers) Ltd.
© Copyright DJ Murphy (Publishers) Ltd.

Printed by Graphicom via dell'Industria – 36100 Vicenza, Italy

ISBN 978-1-913787-06-6

MIX
Paper from responsible sources
FSC® C013123   **RRP £9.99**

The last year turned out to be a little different to the one I had planned, but horses always keep you busy!

Even though travelling overseas was off the cards, I still got to tick off loads from my horsey bucket list. I'd always wanted to visit a top eventer and maybe sit on one of their amazing horses. I got to live that dream when I visited William Fox-Pitt and was able to ride his 5* horse, Little Fire and have a lesson on Cool Mountain – who William rode at WEG in 2010. It was a once in a lifetime experience, and I still can't believe it actually happened!

I took a trip to meet the Fletchers, and they challenged me to ride one of their top showjumpers. It was so cool to see how they run their yard, meet all their beautiful horses, and have a go myself! We had sooo much fun that I've even gone back again since.

Hanging out with Will and Ollie

VOLTAIRE design

The *Mystic* TV show was launched, and oh my goodness it's so brilliant. Macey Chipping aka Issy came to visit my yard, and we even got her to ride Casper. Unbelievably, before filming the show in New Zealand, Macey watched some of my videos to learn more about horses!

Last year I met Lydia Heywood for the first time, and we worked together on an important campaign to raise awareness of racial inequality in our sport. It's a topic I'm passionate about and am trying to help in any way I can with my platform. We also got to go and have some fun at Hickstead with their amazing cross-country course!

You know me, I'm always up for a challenge and last year saw my brother Max take part, too! We had so much fun making our sister vs brother videos, and what you've all been asking for finally happened... we got Max on a horse! I think my favourite challenge was horse vs bike, I can't wait for the chance to film some more soon.

Phew, I think that brings us up to speed with some of my favourite moments! Let's see what this year has in store for us...

ESME'S SHOW GUIDE:

YOUR FIRST SHOWJUMPING COMP

Get ready to smash your first outing over showjumps!

GETTING STARTED

POV: You've nailed jumping a course in your lessons and are looking for your next challenge – a showjumping competition. If you're ready to jump but aren't certain on the details, don't worry – here are my tips to make sure your first comp goes as smoothly as possible.

CHOOSE YOUR VENUE

The best location for your first competition is somewhere you've been before for lessons, schooling or even as a spectator. That way, you'll know how to get there and where everything is. Plus, your pony might have jumped some of the fillers that'll be set up on your competition course, too!

Kit list

As well as all the essentials like my tack, hay and water, here's what I like to pack for Joey before a showjumping competition...

- **stud girth** You guys know I love a stud girth when jumping to keep Joey's tummy safe from his snappy front legs!
- **tendon and fetlock boots** These protect the important structures in Joey's legs
- **plain CC saddlecloth** I use a close contact jump saddle for jumping and I like to go smart for competition – I opt for white, black or navy
- **showjumping whip** Shorter and flatter than a normal short stick so it doesn't get in the way while you're jumping
- **show jacket** I love my snazzy navy jacket for showjumping
- **smart gloves** You know me, I won't get in the saddle without them! I have a dark, fancy pair that I save especially for competition

Top tip

To save time, I like to bath and groom Joey the evening before a competition so all I have to do in the morning is quick touch-ups.

ADD SOME COLOUR?

Are you keen to showcase your favourite colour saddlecloth in your showjumping class? Check with the venue or organiser about any dress code rules – sometimes they're more than happy for you to have a touch of matchy-matchy!

PLAN YOUR DAY

Working out my time of arrival is the first thing I like to do before a show. My first showjumping competition with Joey was part of a combined training outing we did, which includes a dressage test as well, so I had more to plan. The organisers were so helpful, though, and it all went super-smoothly.

The show schedule will often give you a guide to when your class is likely to start, and it's a good idea to have a peep at the entries list online to help you work out what time to be in the collecting ring to warm up, especially if you haven't been given a time slot.

Once you've worked this out, factor in how long it'll take to tack up and drive to the venue after loading your pony and all his kit to give you plenty of time and peace of mind.

ON ARRIVAL

When I get to a show, I like to collect my number, walk the course and then watch a few horses jump so I can get an idea of how other people are tackling it. You can walk the course before you get your pony ready to ride or after you've warmed up with a helper holding him for you – it all depends on your timing. When I walk the course, I always make sure to walk exactly the route I'll take with Joey – it's surprising how deep into the corners I have to ride to make sure he's balanced and on a good line to the fences. I also like to stride out the combinations and related distances with my paces so I know how many strides to expect. Here's a table of how many of my paces make up the different stride patterns for horses and ponies. Ask your instructor to help you work out how many of your paces fit your pony's strides.

Combination strides	Pony distance	Horse distance
1	5.5–8 paces / 5–7m	7–8.5 paces / 6–7.5m
2	9–11 paces / 8.5–10m	11–12.5 paces / 10–11m
3	12–15 paces / 11–13m	15–16 paces / 13.5–14.5m
4	16–19 paces / 14–17m	19–20 paces / 17.5–18.5m ⟫

WARM-UP WISE

Your first port of call is to tell the steward – who should be standing near the collecting ring or by the main arena gate – that you've arrived. They'll tell you how many to go before you or will write your number down in the running order.

Then it's time to loosen your pony up with a good walk, trot and canter in the collecting ring. Ride plenty of transitions and pop a couple of fences on each rein. It can be a busy place, and there are a few rules to follow to keep it safe for everyone...

- **pass left to left** If another rider's approaching you on the other rein, you should pass so that they're on your left side and you're on theirs
- **walk on an inner track** Whether you're just starting to warm up or your pony needs a breather, do your walking just inside of the track so that others working in trot or canter can use it without having to weave around everyone else. Similarly, don't halt on the track as this can cause a pile-up!
- **leave plenty of room** Following other ponies too closely can be dangerous in case they slow down or stop unexpectedly, so always keep a two or three horse distance between your pony and others. Look out for ponies with a red ribbon in their tail as this indicates they might kick
- **be flag-wise** If there are flags either side of the jumps, that means you're supposed to jump them in a particular direction. Always keep a red flag on your right and a white on your left
- **call out before jumping** Don't be shy – call out to let other riders know you're going to jump a fence before you turn to approach it. On landing, ride a straight getaway back to the track

Top tip

Does your pony start his show day a little bit spicy? Give him a walk around the lorry park until he settles down. You can always ask a helper to lead him if you're unsure.

ON COURSE

Time to enter the ring! Here are some key things to remember as you jump your competition round...

- **wait for the bell** A bell or a buzzer will signal to you when it's time to approach fence one. Don't start before you've heard it or you'll be eliminated!
- **focus on your rhythm and route** I try not to get too bogged down with the height of the jumps or if Joey knocks any. Instead, I focus on riding the best I can, following the route I planned in the course walk and making sure Joey's canter doesn't get too speedy

- **take it easy** Joey's still a baby and I want him to have a really positive experience when competing. Even though it means four penalties, I'd always take a circle if he lost his balance or got too quick. It's much better to leave the ring having had fun, so if you're feeling the pressure it's fine to circle and plan your next move

BRING IT ON!

It can be nerve-wracking going in to jump a course, but the best thing you can do is concentrate on 10/10 technique – and enjoy the moment! As ever, focus on all the things that went amazingly, not just your pony's performance in the main arena, and anything that didn't go to plan is just an area to improve next time!

MY WARDROBE

When I'm not editing videos I'm with the horses, so I need kit that's going to keep me comfortable and safe – and it's all the better when it looks great, too!

ROAD RIDER

When I'm heading out for a hack the most important thing is that other road and bridleway users can see me coming. If they know where I am, they're way more likely to slow down and pass me in a sensible place. My absolute fave top for hacking out is this high-vis and reflective baselayer. It has all the safety features of a high-vis vest or jacket without the bulk. I like to team it with some neutral breeches or riding tights that won't pick up the dirt and a high-vis hat band to wear over the top of my skull cap.

ALL TERRAIN

Going cross-country is one of Casper's all-time favourite things to do – and it seems Joey's a big fan, too! While there's nothing better than going for a blast and challenging yourself over some natural fences, cross-country riding requires some serious safety gear. The most important thing, as always, is your safety helmet. When choosing a hat to wear for cross-country you'll need one that's fitted correctly, doesn't have a fixed peak and meets the latest safety standards. A skull cap's perfect. You can either opt for a coloured helmet, like this one, or choose a brightly coloured hat silk to go on top – or both!

A body protector is the next must-wear item for cross-country. Again, it's really important that it fits properly in order for it to protect you. You'll find all good tack shops have qualified fitters who can help you find the right size and fit. For safety helmets and body protectors, it's super-important to replace them if you have a fall, because the features that protect you may be damaged and not offer the same protection as they're designed to the next time.

The next bit of my cross-country kit is the fun part – a brightly coloured baselayer. I've gone for this vibrant turquoise that not only matches my helmet but Joey's saddle pad, too!

> *It might look like I have a glamorous lifestyle on my videos, but the reality is I'm doing lots of jobs around the yard every day*

COMPETITION READY

I get so excited on competition days that I can't wait to get into all my gear, but it's a good idea to put a tracksuit over the top as white breeches and horses don't always mix! I like to ride in a crisp white pair of breeches with a full silicone seat for extra stickability in the saddle – just in case! I match this with a cool and breathable stock shirt – this one is my favourite and has a grey front panel, which is so pretty. Because I love my showjumping, I've chosen a short show jacket that has silver zipped pockets and matching silver piping on the collar. It's made from a stretchy, water-resistant fabric and it's so comfy I could ride in it all day!

WORK IT!

My life might look glamorous in the videos, but the reality is I'm doing lots of jobs around the yard every day and sometimes I just have to get my hands dirty. This pair of overalls has come into its own time and time again, whether I'm cleaning out the water troughs, painting the stables or just watering the plants – it's just so practical.

SCHOOL CHIC

Like most riders, I probably spend at least half of my riding time in the arena – so it's essential that I'm comfortable and that the kit I use is up to the job. Lots of people school in short boots and gaiters or chaps, but I much prefer the feeling I get in long boots. I like to wear neutral-coloured breeches with a silicone seat and I usually team these with a plain belt. On top I love to wear bright colours, but the most important thing to me is that I'm comfy. I always choose technical fabrics that will help to keep me at the right temperature come rain or shine. This pretty helmet, which meets all the current safety standards, is one of my favourites – it's really comfortable, and has a rose gold trim and a fixed peak.

puzzle fun

WORDSEARCH

Can you find all the words hidden in this puzzle?

```
C O R J E G N I T S U O J I
R E S N E I M H N W A L K S
O D B A N Y L I U L N S O O
S R R R D I L V O M T T N W
S E A E U O S T R N N O A S
C S T T R U R O U E B R R I
O S A E A M N R P D D R C V
U A C V N P C T L R Y A H H
N G H E C S L N O U I C E G
T E A V E J J B G M I E R I
R C C A N T E R B P I R Y H
Y M O U N T E D G A M E S M
T C E S G R I D W O R K E V
B O G N I P M U J W O H S L
```

- ⊘ Dressage
- ⊘ Showjumping
- ⊘ Cross-country
- ⊘ Gridwork
- ① High vis
- ⊘ Wardrobe
- ⊘ Endurance
- ⊘ Mounted games
- ⊘ Archery
- ⊘ Jousting
- ⊘ Veteran
- ⊘ Walk
- ⊘ Trot
- ⊘ Canter
- ⊘ Carrots

Turn to page 100 for the answers!

SPOT THE DIFFERENCE IIII I

Can you spot all six changes to this picture of me with Paralympic legend and fellow Brooke supporter, Natasha Baker?

Did you know?
Natasha has won an incredible five gold Paralympic medals

Meeting Natasha was so inspiring – especially seeing the way her horses respond to her voice

This Esme's
RAD ROUTINES
SPRING

The grass is growing, the birds are singing and the horses are loving some sunshine – spring must be here! There's always plenty to be done, so check out what the equines and I get up to...

CLEAN IT UP
Spring's the perfect time for me to get some deep-cleaning done and give the yard – and horses – a spruce-up. From scrubbing buckets and de-cobwebbing stables, to bathing and trimming your pony, there's always masses to be done. The warmer weather and longer days provide the perfect opportunity, too.

SPIN ME RIGHT ROUND
It's time to rotate our fields to give the winter paddocks a good rest and make sure that everyone has plenty of new grass to eat. However, it's super-important to make sure they don't pack on the pounds with all the fresh grass coming through!

ALL RUGGED UP
With winter out of the way, spring is when I give my heavy turnout rugs a really thorough clean so they're ready to go as soon as the weather turns at the end of the year. That way, I know I'm mega-prepared way in advance and don't have to worry about them in autumn.

FULL TUMMY
With the grass coming through – and my paddocks all freshly rotated – it's sooo important to keep a close eye on all my equines' weights. I call the Baileys Nutrition Line to see if I need to make any gradual adjustments to their diets.

TACK ATTACK
We all love buying second-hand – it's great for your purse and the planet! Tack sales are an awesome way to clear out all the things I no longer need, such as old bits or rugs that don't fit anymore. I always make sure they're in decent condition and give them a quick clean before selling them – nobody wants to buy muddy brushing boots!

Add your springtime jobs to my list below...

spring cleaning ☐

rotate fields ☐

wash rugs ☐

sell old gear ☐

check my pony's diet ☐

.... ☐

.... ☐

.... ☐

.... ☐

.... ☐

.... ☐

.... ☐

.... ☐

> **"Spring's the perfect time of year for me to get some serious deep-cleaning done"**

HORSEBACK ARCHERY

I had so much fun with the Knights of Middle England learning how to shoot arrows from on board a cantering horse – here's why I think you should give it a try!

If you've ever seen *Brave, Lord of the Rings* or any action film with a medieval setting, you're bound to have come across horseback archery before. I bet you've secretly always wanted to try it – I know I have! That's why I was so excited to spend a day learning how to do it as one of my *Challenge Esme* videos. It was such an amazing experience and I felt so free cantering around with no reins while shooting arrows!

Fancy giving it a go but unsure about the details? Here's what I got up to when I became a trainee horseback archer.

> "I felt so free cantering around with no reins while shooting arrows!"

Jargon buster

- **Corridor** – a thin section of the arena cordoned off by barriers to keep a horse cantering straight while arrows are shot
- **Pile** – the pointy end of the arrow
- **Nock** – the clip at the opposite end of the arrow that sits in the bow string
- **Bullseye** – the small, central circle of a target
- **Shooting barebow** – shooting arrows from a bow that has no notches or rests to guide the arrow

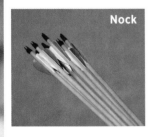
Nock

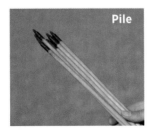
Pile

What will I need?

Archery isn't something you can really try at home, but there places that offer experience days. They'll provide bows, arrows, targets and horses for you – just bring yourself, your hat, gloves and riding boots. I found that a glove was really useful for holding the bow, but I loaded the arrows with a gloveless hand. It's quite fiddly, and I could feel what I was doing better without a glove. »

Feet on the ground

I was desperate to get onto a horse and start shooting, but the first task in horse archery is to learn to shoot an arrow on the ground. It was definitely harder than I was expecting, but I managed to get an arrow right in the bullseye eventually! I was shooting barebow, which means there are no notches to guide the arrow – I just had a piece of tape at the front of the bow to help me align it. Then, I was shown how to place the arrow onto the bow, taking care when handling the sharp pile that faced the target, and clip the nock onto the bowstring.

How to draw

The pile sits on top of your thumb and your forefinger curls around the top of it. Then, you slide your hand down the bow and clip the nock into the string. There's a traditional technique used in horse archery called thumb draw. To do this, curl in your middle, ring and little fingers, then wrap your thumb around the string and press the tip of your thumb into the knuckle of your middle finger. Bring your index finger round to sit lightly on your thumbnail. Draw the arrow back and relax your fingers as you release the arrow.

Mastering the thumb draw

Saddle up

Once the ground training's complete, the next step is to take it onto horseback. After my horse, Freddie, and I had warmed up, we moved on to shooting some arrows from a standstill to settle in. That wasn't too tricky, so we progressed to walking down the corridor. It was still pretty easy to load the arrows as Freddie's walk was smooth and steady, but my advice is to be ready for how fast the targets come up on a moving horse – I certainly wasn't! Before you know what's happening you've ridden past them and I actually shot quite a few of my arrows too late, so it's definitely wise to plan well ahead. Because you shoot the arrows while standing up in your stirrups, it's also a real test of your balance and something that takes a few goes to perfect.

On the move

Oh my goodness, there's so much to think about when you start trotting! Not only do you have to rise to the trot, you're also moving around a lot more with the bouncy movement, so loading the bow becomes really fiddly as you're trying to get your fingers in the right place. Planning ahead becomes even more important here as the targets whizz by! I had to adjust my aim because a lot of my arrows flew straight over the top of the targets. I also had to remember to keep using my leg, as Freddie did occasionally sneak in a cheeky walk break. It was definitely an in-depth lesson in multi-tasking, but I was so proud every time I managed to hit the target that I couldn't help but have a little celebration.

Success is being on the target!

Wild and free

Pretty soon it was time to try a canter. I couldn't believe how confident I was cantering Freddie without reins. The horses who are trained in horseback archery are so well schooled and know their job inside-out, so you can be sure they're going to stick within the corridor and give you a smooth ride.

The feeling of cantering around without any reins, carrying a bow and shooting at targets is honestly the most amazing and empowering experience! Even if I hadn't managed to hit any targets, I think I still wouldn't have been able to stop smiling. Coming away from a fantastic day out, knowing that I'd hit a target with an arrow while cantering a horse – and with video evidence – is absolutely unbeatable. I'd definitely recommend having a go at archery on horseback to anyone.

LOOK HIS *best*

Practise your plaiting skills and get your pony looking his best as Joey and I run you through our step-by-step guide

Mane attraction

1. Comb your pony's mane to make sure it's tangle-free. It's helpful to dampen it with a sponge or use a plaiting spray to keep it neat.
2. Divide his mane into an odd number of evenly sized sections. I use a mane comb to make sure they're all the same width. Secure each section with a plaiting band.
3. Split the first section into three smaller ones, making sure they're even. Then, plait it to the end – don't forget to keep it tight!
4. Use a plaiting band to secure the bottom of the plait.
5. Once you've done the same to the rest of the sections, start folding each plait up into a neat ball.
6. Roll them as tightly as possible and secure each one with another plaiting band.

Top tip

You could plait your pony's forelock just like you do his mane, or in a French plait as you do his tail, which looks extra fancy!

Tail end

1. Starting at the top of your pony's tail, dampen the hair and take three small sections – two from one side of the tail and one from the other.
2. Plait down the tail, pulling extra sections in as you go – like a French plait. Try to keep it as tight as possible, and make all the sections the same size.
3. Once you get roughly three-quarters of the way down his dock, carry on plaiting the hair you have without bringing any extra sections in.

4. Secure with a plaiting band, then double it over by tucking the braid under itself and putting on another band.

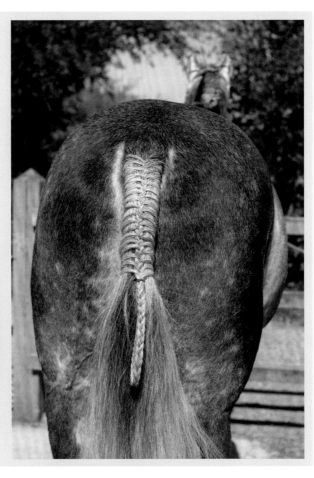

Roll the plaits as tightly as possible and secure them with a plaiting band

Sooo smart!

Trim and tidy

I like to trim my horses' hair to make them look super-smart. I usually trim their...

- **ears**, by folding them closed and cutting any protruding hairs that stick out with scissors
- **bridle path**, trimming a section at the poll where the headpiece sits to make it more comfortable and neat
- **jaw and fetlocks** using a set of trimmers or a comb and scissors to make sure they're neat and tidy
  You don't have to trim your pony – I love the natural look on Mickey! One thing I'd never ever trim is the horses' whiskers – they need these to help with their senses.

Make a donkey keyring

Oh my goodness, these are so cute and absolutely perfect to make sure I always know where my keys are

let's get started

What you'll need:
- pencil/pen
- template from page 101
- grey or brown felt
- white felt
- scissors
- needle
- embroidery thread
- keyring loop
- glue
- toy stuffing

Top tip

If your sewing's a bit wobbly you could use a pen to draw on the face instead of using a running stitch.

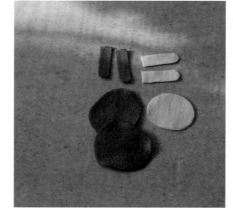

1

Using a pencil or pen, draw around the face and ear templates onto your grey or brown felt – you'll need two of each. Next, draw around the muzzle and ear template on the white felt – this time you only need two ears and one muzzle. Cut out all of the pieces.

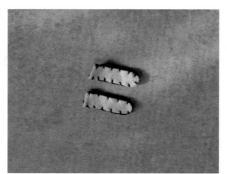

2

To make the ears you need to overlay a white ear on top of a grey or brown ear and blanket stitch these together using your thread. Repeat, so that you end up with two, neatly stitched ears.

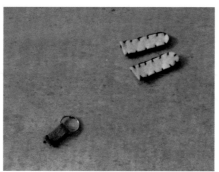

3

Next, cut a rectangle of grey or brown felt to create the loop attachment for the keyring. Thread it through the ring and secure with a few stitches.

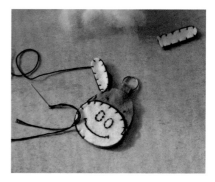

4 Use a running stitch to create the nostrils and smile on your white muzzle – you can mark it out with a pencil or pen before you stitch to keep you on the right track. Now, blanket stitch the top half of the muzzle shape. Once you've done that, glue the muzzle onto the face piece. Next, use a simple running stitch to make some eyes just above the muzzle.

5 Now it's time to assemble your keyring. Place the two head sections one on top of the other with the sewn features facing out. Use a blanket stitch to sew them together, making sure you start at the bottom and work your way up. When you get near to the top, you need to insert the first ear – sandwiching it in-between the front and back pieces of the head. Make sure you have the white part of the ear facing the front and use a running stitch to secure it in place.

6 Continue with the blanket stitch until you reach the very top, then add in the keyring loop just as you did the first ear. Don't forget to add in the second ear as you start to make your way back down the other side of your donkey's head using your blanket stitch.

7 Before you get all the way back to the start, you need to add a little bit of stuffing. Try to make sure it's evenly spread out inside. Once you're happy with the amount of stuffing, continue with a blanket stitch and secure at the bottom where you started.

Make one for each set of keys

Dreams
CAN COME TRUE

Discover how to reach your riding goals

t's important to always have targets for your riding, as that way you can keep on improving! Whether you want to ride your first canter or jump a clear round showjumping, I share with you the ways I like to plan ahead, so you can achieve your dreams!

LOVELY LISTS

First things first, you need to figure out what your goals are going to be. I'm talking your biggest endgame dreams! Pick up to three things, so you don't have too many to focus on all at once. Do you want to win at a one-day event, or ace riding a 20m circle? However big or small yours are, list them below!

MY TOP THREE GOALS

1. To jump bigger than 50cm

I want to achieve this by... 2023

2. To have my own horse

I want to achieve this by... the end of my life

3.

I want to achieve this by...

SET A TIMER

Now you know what your main riding goals are, you need to set yourself a time limit to achieve them in. Do you want to have completed them in a year, six months, one month? You can allocate a different deadline to each of your goals. Just make sure it's going to be safe and achievable for you to do.

BABY STEPS

Thinking about achieving your goals may feel like a daunting task, but don't worry! You don't need to take massive leaps right away. One of mine is to enter a 90cm showjumping class with Joey. So, the way I can get there will be...

☐ Jump a related distance at 85cm

☐ Jump a grid with one fence at 90cm

☐ Jump a full course of 85cm at home

☐ Compete in an 80cm showjumping class

☐ Jump a course of 95cm at home

☐ Compete in a 90cm showjumping class!

Goal achieved!

Now you try...

MY STEPS

☐ _____

☐ _____

☐ _____

☐ _____

☐ _____

☐ _____

Goal achieved:

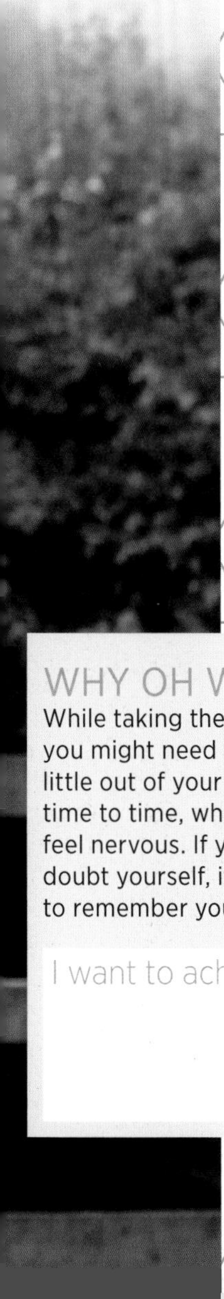

WHY OH WHY?

While taking these smaller steps, you might need to push yourself a little out of your comfort zone from time to time, which can make you feel nervous. If you're beginning to doubt yourself, it's super-important to remember your why! Why do you want to achieve these goals? Is it so you can become a better rider? Become an instructor one day? Go for fun hacks with your friends without feeling nervous? Whatever your why, make sure you remember it so you never give up!

I want to achieve my goals because...

STICK IT OUT

I never said achieving your dreams was going to be easy! You'll need to put in the hard work and stay determined. Just remember, you can achieve anything you put your mind to!

With these guys in my life, the highs always outnumber the lows

A TO Z
OF VETERAN PONIES

I've owned Mickey for 11 years now and in that time he's entered into his senior years. Here's my guide for what to look out for as ponies get a little older

A IS FOR ARTHRITIS

Lots of older ponies will develop some degree of arthritis as they age, which can cause reduced flexibility, stiffness or a shortened stride. Your vet will be able to help you decide on the right steps to take, and give guidance on your pony's exercise, medication and supplements, too.

B IS FOR BODY CONDITION SCORING

This method of assessing your pony's body fat by rating it from 1–5 or 1–10 is a great way to monitor his overall condition and make sure he's not too fat or too thin. Areas ponies tend to hold extra weight on include their crest, shoulder, ribs and hindquarters.

C IS FOR CUDDLES

You might find that you aren't able to do as much with your veteran pony as you used to – but there's nothing to stop you spoiling him with cuddles! Mickey's 100% as licky as ever and I love giving him lots and lots of hugs.

D IS FOR DEGENERATIVE JOINT DISEASE (DJD)

DJD is a common cause of lameness and affects horses of all ages – but as it's a form of arthritis, it's more common in veterans. DJD isn't curable, but vets and farriers can make affected horses more comfortable.

This Esme

E IS FOR EYES

Some horses develop cataracts as they age. This is a clouding of the lens, which can impact a horse's vision and will need to be diagnosed by a vet. Partially sighted horses require careful handling – especially while they adapt to their new way of life.

F IS FOR FLUFFY

Horses look super-cute with their winter coats, but older ponies who struggle to shed them or have extremely long coats could be suffering from PPID. Ask your yard owner if you have concerns about your pony's coat.

G IS FOR GREYING

You certainly won't spot it on Mickey, but did you know older horses can start to grey just like humans? This normally starts around the eyes, muzzle and ears.

Super fluffy!

H IS FOR HERD

As ponies grow older, their place in the herd pecking order may change. Keep a close eye on your pony's relationship with his fieldmates as he ages and consider moving him to a herd with other older ponies if he looks like he may enjoy a slower paced life.

I IS FOR IN-HAND

Just because you can no longer ride your pony, it doesn't mean the fun has to stop! Mickey absolutely loves in-hand work – either being lunged or playing chase in the school. I even take Mickey out hacking on the lead rein when the weather's nice!

J IS FOR JUMPING

There might come a time when you decide to stop jumping your older pony, but you can still put your equipment to good use. Try using poles to mark out a maze for him to walk through or using jump wings as bending poles.

K IS FOR KEEPING UP

Some horses start to find it difficult to carry on at the same pace as their hacking buddies. If you find you're getting left behind when you go for a canter, ask them to slow down or try to find another friend with a steadier pony to ride out with instead. »

L IS FOR LOSS OF CONDITION

A sudden loss of condition is a cause for concern for all ponies, but especially so when they get older. It can be a sign there are dental or digestion problems and the best course of action is to consult your vet.

M IS FOR MELANOMAS

Older grey or cremello horses, like Mickey, are prone to melanomas. They appear as small black spherical lumps, but can grow and change colour. Most are harmless, at least to begin with, but it's important to monitor them as they can change over time.

N IS FOR NUTRITION

Your pony's nutritional needs may change as he gets older and the best thing you can do is call a feedline, such as the Baileys Nutrition Line, and ask a professional what he needs to stay healthy.

O IS FOR OLD AGE

Lots of people say that the first five years of a horse's life is the equivalent of 23 human years. After that, each year is roughly the equivalent to 2.5 human years. That makes Mickey around 70 years old – so it's not surprising he's not really missing being ridden every day!

P IS FOR PITUITARY PARS INTERMEDIA DYSFUNCTION (PPID)

Often referred to as Cushing's disease, PPID occurs when the pituitary gland develops a tumour, which causes excessive production of hormones. Signs a pony has PPID include lethargy, developing a longer coat, failing to shed their winter coat in spring, sweating, laminitis and weight loss. There are several treatments for PPID, so speak to your vet if you suspect your pony may be suffering from it.

Q IS FOR QUARTERLY HEALTH CHECKS

It's really helpful to keep a record of your pony's weight, body condition score and any changing ailments, and update it every three months. That way, you can spot gradual changes and get your vet involved if you need to.

R IS FOR RETIREMENT

Lots of ponies are ridden well into their 20s, and some even longer, but there may come a time when you feel your pony's ready to slow down and have an easier life. I stopped riding Mickey a few years ago, but we still have loads of fun together.

S IS FOR SOAKED FEEDS

For older horses with poor teeth, soaking feeds can make them much easier to digest. It can also help increase their water intake.

T IS FOR TEETH

As horses age, their incisor teeth can get very long – or they could become unevenly worn and eventually wear right down to the gums, which will make it hard for them to eat. Because of this, it's really important that older equines see a vet or qualified equine dental technician every six months. They'll be able to rasp rough edges when needed and let you know about any important changes in your pony's mouth – like wobbly molars.

U IS FOR URINATING

If you notice your pony's starting to wee more than usual, it's time to call the vet. Increased urination can be a sign of PPID or other old-age related conditions.

V IS FOR VETERAN

Just like people, horses are living for longer and enjoying a better quality of life – so becoming a veteran doesn't necessarily mean the end of competitions. There are classes especially for older equines, including ridden and in-hand showing, and veteran dressage.

W IS FOR WEIGHT

Like all horses, older ones are best kept at a healthy weight. Becoming overweight makes them more susceptible to PPID – which is why I always measure Mickey's feeds and use a small holed haynet to slow his eating. If your pony finds it harder to hold onto his weight, you may need to increase the amount of forage and feed you offer him.

X IS FOR EXCESSIVE DRINKING

It's super-important to monitor how much an older pony drinks each day because excessive drinking can be a sign of poor health. Always call your vet if you're worried.

Y IS FOR YOUNGSTERS

Despite the fact that Mickey and Joey are the best of friends, some older ponies get to a stage in life where they no longer want to be turned out with playful youngsters. Keep an eye on the dynamics of your pony's herd – older ponies are usually very good at letting you know when they've had enough!

Z IS FOR ZZZZS

Sleep is important for equines of all ages, but there are a few things you need to look out for in veterans. If your pony's struggling to get up and down, or isn't as speedy as he used to be, it could be because he's reluctant to sleep lying down in the field. This can make horses irritable and spooky. Giving your older pony a safe place to catch some serious Zzzzs can help.

5 MINUTES
with Duke

What Duke would say if he opened up in a Q&A

How old were you when you were rescued?
I was just a few days old when I was found abandoned on a Welsh hillside in 2020.

What happened to you?
No one knows why I was there all by myself, but luckily I was rescued by the team at World Horse Welfare. They took me to Glenda Spooner Farm and hand-reared me, bottle feeding me the milk I should've received from my own mother.

How tall will you grow?
It's hard to say exactly without knowing what either of my parents were like, but the experts at World Horse Welfare think I'll probably be around 11hh.

Were you excited to meet your new family?
I'd lived at Glenda Spooner Farm almost my whole life, so when I found out I was being rehomed by Esme I was sooo excited, but also quite nervous. I'm really lucky that I've got Mickey, though – he's awesome at showing me the ropes and we're such good friends, already!

What colour are you?
I'm grey. I started off almost black but now you can see some dapples peeking through my coat.

What breed are you?
I'm a Welsh Mountain Pony.

What's your favourite pastime?
Galloping about and sleeping. I've got loads more growing to do – which takes lots of energy – so nap time's the best!

Will you ever be ridden?
Maybe! There's no reason why not, but I was only born in 2020 so I'm not ready yet!

35

Make a painted rock photo holder

I love surrounding myself with pictures of all my pets and these holders make them even more personal

let's get started

What you'll need:
- flat smooth rocks
- three colours of acrylic paint or paint pens
- paintbrush
- templates of Joey and Mickey from page 101
- scissors
- pen/pencil
- copper wire

Top tip

If you can't find any suitable rocks or pebbles in your garden, try your local garden centre.

1

Select your rocks carefully – the smoother and flatter the better. Give them a good wash, making sure you remove any dirt and leave them to dry.

2

Next use a paintbrush and acrylic paint or paint pens to give your rocks a background colour. Make sure they dry completely before moving on to the next step.

3

You can cut out the templates of Joey and Mickey on page 101 or draw a silhouette of your own. Use a pen or pencil to mark around the templates, then fill them in with paint or paint pens.

4 Now you can add some extra decoration. I've gone for hearts and stars.

5 You could experiment with different rocks, and change up the colours.

6 Cut a length of copper wire, that will easily wrap around the rock a couple of times and then stand up. Coil one end of the wire around a pen three or four times to create your photo holder. Wrap the other end around the rock leaving about 10cm sticking up to hold your photos.

Love you x

This Esme's
RAD ROUTINES
SUMMER

I just LOVE summer – tonnes of riding and best of all, loads of ice cream! There's plenty you'll need to do for your pony alongside all the fun you'll have – here's what I get up to...

BUZZ OFF!

Getting great fly protection is super-important to keep the equines comfy during the summer. I make sure they all have a fly mask and rug, plus plenty of fly spray on hand to keep those biting insects at bay. Mickey often comes into his stable to avoid the worst of the heat and the flies, particularly because he's prone to getting a sunburnt nose!

WEIGHT WATCHING

Just like in the spring, it's sooo important to keep an eye on the horses' weights through the summer. While they're working really hard practising for all the fun stuff we have planned, that doesn't mean they can't still pile on the pounds. I weightape all of the equines every week to make sure they stay trim and healthy for all their cool activities.

IN THE DIARY

Summer's always packed full of awesome shows, clinics, fun rides and days out to enjoy with the ponies – so I try to get plenty booked in! I make a plan of what I want to fit in through the season, then I can make sure I'm well-prepared and the ponies are fit.

JOB LOT

There's never any shortage of jobs to be getting on with in between riding and bonding sessions with the ponies! It's the perfect time of year to pull the rubber mats out of the stables and give it all a thorough clean. The warm sun helps everything dry quickly, too.

WASHING UP

By this time of year the horsebox is in need of a good scrub. I love to give it a bit of TLC while the sun's out, and it gives me the chance to make sure everything's in good working order so the horses can travel safely, too.

Add your summertime jobs to my list below...

- [ ] fly protection
- [ ] show schedule
- [ ] weightaping
- [ ] scrub the stable
- [ ] check and clean transport
- [ ] ....
- [ ] ....
- [ ] ....
- [ ] ....
- [ ] ....
- [ ] ....
- [ ] ....
- [ ] ....

"There's never any shortage of jobs to be getting on with in between riding and bonding sessions"

YOUR FIRST DRESSAGE TEST

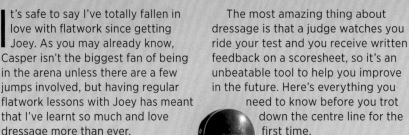

What's better than getting dressed up and dancing like no one's watching?
In a dressage competition you can take your pony, too!

It's safe to say I've totally fallen in love with flatwork since getting Joey. As you may already know, Casper isn't the biggest fan of being in the arena unless there are a few jumps involved, but having regular flatwork lessons with Joey has meant that I've learnt so much and love dressage more than ever.

The most amazing thing about dressage is that a judge watches you ride your test and you receive written feedback on a scoresheet, so it's an unbeatable tool to help you improve in the future. Here's everything you need to know before you trot down the centre line for the first time.

PICK A TEST

First up is choosing a dressage test. Think about what you do at home and in your lessons – are you happy to canter in your test, or would one where you only have to walk and trot be a better option? Speak to your instructor about your plans and they should be able to help.

You're allowed to have your test called on the day, which is super-helpful if you're feeling the pressure, but it's still important to learn and practise the movements. That being said, there is such a thing as being over-prepared! It's best to ride through your test a couple of times, maybe in a lesson, but then just practise parts of it. This is because your pony might catch on and learn the test, too, and start anticipating the movements. Worse yet, he could get bored and that means he won't bring his A game on the big day!

How do you get around this? Well, it's super-fun to practise your test on foot, too! You can even set up a makeshift school in the garden or on the yard and run through the test as if you were on your pony. Why not get your yard friends involved and have a competition of your own?

Top tip
Dressage arenas are marked out with white boards in the corners and along the sides. Ponies can sometimes find these spooky, so it's good to go somewhere you can practise with them to desensitise your pony.

Kit list

Here's what I bring with me for a dressage comp on top of all the essentials like my tack, hay and water...

- **dressage-legal bit** Did you know there are rules on what bit you can use in a dressage competition? I'm lucky enough that Joey wears a snaffle at all times, which I'm allowed to compete in, but if you're not sure about your pony's bit ask your instructor or yard owner for help
- **white dressage square** I have a fancy one that only comes out for competitions!
- **long whip** So that I don't have to take my hands off the reins to use it if I need to
- **stain remover** Dressage is all about looking as smart as possible! You guys know my grey horses just love to get mucky, so I always keep stain remover handy for any last minute touch-ups
- **white gloves** Again, I have an extra-special show pair, but you can wear your normal ones, or dark gloves if you prefer
- **show jacket** My smart navy jacket completes the look

Did you know?
If you ever see a ribbon in a pony's tail at a show, it has a meaning! Red means the pony kicks, green means he's young or inexperienced and white means he's a stallion.

ON THE DAY

One of the amazing things about dressage is that you'll be given a time for your test – no guesswork involved! This makes it super-easy to work out how much time you'll need to arrive, inform the steward you're there, grab your number and warm up.

The warm-up is your last chance to have a sneaky practise of any elements of your test you find tricky, so use your time wisely to get in the zone. If you warm up your pony in boots, ask your helper to take them off for you before you head into the ring, as they're not allowed to be worn during your test. »

TEST TIME

It's time to go in! Here are some important things to remember...

- **wait before you go** Just like in a showjumping competition, you'll be told when to start by a buzzer, bell or sometimes a car horn. While you wait, settle your pony around the edge of the dressage boards. Lots of people just like to trot round, but do whatever feels right – he might prefer to walk or benefit from a little canter to wake him up. I always start on Joey's better rein, the left, as this gives me a cleaner turn onto the centre line
- **make sure he's ready** The car horn I mentioned? This is used as a signal to start as judges often watch from their cars. It's a good idea to introduce your pony to the sound before you go to a show, whether that's from a real car horn or a clip on YouTube
- **don't be afraid of mistakes** Nothing always goes perfectly to plan, and even the world's best riders can feel disappointed if they don't perform a movement quite as well as they wanted. They even go wrong sometimes, which loses them marks. However, they don't let that feeling influence how they ride for the rest of the test, and neither should you! If you do make a mistake, the judge will usually beep their horn again and you go back to the previous movement before carrying on where you left off.

SCORESHEETS EXPLAINED

Confused by what's on your scoresheet? Each movement gets a mark out of 10 and some, like free walk, receive two times the marks – so the score you get for that particular movement is doubled! The judge will sometimes note down why you got the mark you did, which is invaluable to take to your future schooling sessions.

You also receive marks for how you and your pony went overall, called collective marks. These are also out of 10, and you receive them for your pony's...

- **paces** A regular rhythm will boost your marks
- **impulsion** This is about your pony moving forward, listening to your leg and feeling energetic without being too speedy, which means he'll be powering himself along from his back legs
- **submission** The judge will be looking for your pony to be relaxed, moving freely and listening to you
- **position and seat** Head up, heels down, shoulders back – all the things that make a good position will be rewarded here!
- **effectiveness of aids** This means that when you ask for your pony to speed up, slow down or turn, you produce the desired result

JUDGING, BUT NOT JUDGING

Although a dressage judge will evaluate how you're doing, they're not there to be negative. It can feel like a challenge to have your riding exposed to a critical eye, but all the judge wants is to encourage and reward you, not take marks away. The extra-special thing about your scoresheet? There's always a box at the end for the judge to make some final comments and they're always really inspiring. That's a feeling that can't be beaten – FACT!

Next-level RIDER EXERCISES

Even though I'm around horses nearly 24/7 it's still important to keep myself fit for riding. Here are some of my favourite exercises

PLANK

WHY? The plank exercise is excellent for improving core strength, which will really help me stay balanced and strong in the saddle.

HOW TO DO IT:
Placing my hands on the floor so they're directly underneath my shoulders, I try to keep my body in a straight line from shoulder to heel and hold for the count of 20. If my wrists start to hurt, I drop down onto my elbows instead – this time keeping my elbow directly below my shoulder. I aim to do three reps and I've built up from holding for 20 seconds at a time when I first started, to one minute now that I'm stronger.

SHOULDER TAPS

WHY? This dynamic stretch really tests the strength of my core as I move my arms but try to keep still through my body. I know it's working, but it's sooo tough!

HOW TO DO IT:
Building on the plank pose, I lift one hand and tap the opposite shoulder, then replace. Next, I lift the other hand and tap its opposite shoulder. I try to think about whether my weight's even in both feet, while my hips and torso stay super-still. I do 10 taps each side and repeat four times.

SUPERMAN

WHY? This exercise is great for improving the strength in my back and boosting flexibility.

HOW TO DO IT:
I start by laying on my tummy with legs and arms outstretched. Concentrating on engaging my core, I slowly lift my head, arms and chest while lifting my legs, too. I keep my stomach muscles switched on to support me while I count to five, then gently lower my arms, legs and chest. Repeat 10-15 times.

DEEP SQUATS

WHY? Squats are a great way to strengthen my glutes and hamstrings, which is essential for keeping me safe in the saddle.

HOW TO DO IT:
With my feet spaced a little over hip width apart, I lower my bottom as far as I can and keep my back straight – folding forward at the hip and keeping my toes facing forwards. I aim for three sets of 10 squats.

I know it's working – but it's sooo tough!

LEG RAISES

WHY? These leg raises will help with hip mobility and strengthen the glute muscles.

HOW TO DO IT:
Laying on one side, I prop myself up on the underneath elbow, using the top hand to stabilise me. I gently lift my upper leg, making sure the toe faces forward and down, then lower and repeat 10-15 times. Next I pulse for the count of five – with three reps on each side.

TOE TAPS

WHY? This dynamic exercise builds on the leg lift, but encourages me to switch on my core muscles to stabilise my body while I work the glute.

HOW TO DO IT:
Starting in the leg raiser position, I lift the top leg and then move it forward in an arc shape until I can tap my toe on the floor in front of me. Then I move my leg back in an arc – so that it goes through the starting position and taps the ground behind my resting leg.

MARCHING OUT

Walking is as simple as putting one foot in front of the other, but with horses there's more to it – like two extra feet for starters! With a little help from my fave matchy-matchy bandages, Casper will show you all...

TO THE BEAT
Walk is a four-beat gait which means each foot hits the ground at a different time.

1 2
3 4

Did you know?
There are four types of walk.

MEDIUM WALK

The first walk you'll be asked to perform in dressage tests is medium walk. In this gait, your pony should be walking forwards with purpose and his hind hoof print should fall in front of the print left by his foreleg – this is known as an overtrack. In medium walk, your pony should be marching forwards and working in an outline with a soft contact.

Pitter patter

In walk, the sequence your horse moves his feet in is...
- left hind
- left fore
- right hind
- right fore

In walk, the horse should have at least one foot on the floor at any given time so that there's no moment of suspension.

FREE WALK

In free walk your horse should have a long and low outline, stretching down towards the ground with his nose. He should keep the same rhythm but take longer steps and lengthen through his whole frame. I sometimes find it tempting to have a breather during free walk in a dressage test, but it's important to keep riding forwards and make sure your pony's attention stays on you.

COLLECTED AND EXTENDED WALKS

These next-level walks don't feature in dressage until the harder tests – so don't worry if you and your pony aren't ready to try them just yet.

In an extended walk, the horse is asked to show his maximum overtrack with his head and neck in a longer frame. Collected walk is the opposite – the footprints from his hind feet may fall behind those of his front feet as he uses his hocks to create a powerful and more elevated walk step while maintaining his outline.

Did you know?

In dressage, walk movements earn you double marks – so they're definitely worth practising!

HAVE A GO AT...

ENDURANCE

For some, it's considered the ultimate test of horsemanship with riders partnering their horses for up to 160km. I'd never tried endurance before, but believe it or not, Mickey used to do lots with his previous owner. Find out how I got on when I tried my hand at endurance riding with Beth Langley and her 2018 WEG horse, Tizzy.

How it all began

People have been riding horses to cover long distances ever since they were first domesticated, but it wasn't until the 1950s when endurance became a competitive sport. The first organised ride was from Lake Tahoe to Auburn, across the Sierra Nevada Range in under 24 hours. This challenging ride of 100 miles in high altitude and temperatures of 37°C remains one of the toughest endurance rides, and is known as the Tevis Cup.

What to look for in an endurance horse

Arabs and part-bred Arabs are the most commonly used breeds, but you can have a go on almost any type of horse. It's essential that they're sound as there are strict vet inspections, and even at the lower levels you cover a lot of uneven terrain. It also helps if they're responsive and well behaved. You're going to be in the saddle for a long time, so you don't want a horse that constantly pulls, or spooks at everything!

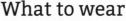

What to wear

For you...

You must wear a current safety standard helmet – but other than that you can pretty much wear what you want. Most riders choose riding tights and crossover boots, which are easy to run in, as well as being comfy for riding. Half chaps and long socks are popular, too, and it's recommended that you wear a long-sleeved top.

For your pony...

Endurance tack is made from biothane instead of leather. This is a tough material made from webbing, which is covered in plastic so that it isn't damaged by the regular water sloshing from the crew. At the top level, endurance horses have to carry a minimum of 75kg, which includes the tack and rider. To avoid the horse having to carry a dead weight, riders like Beth opt for heavier saddles to make up the difference between them and the minimum weight allowance.

Endurance bridles look just like a headcollar that has cheekpieces and a bit clipped onto it. This is because riders don't want to waste precious seconds untacking their horses before the vetting stage of the competition – so they just whip the saddle off and unclip the bit. To make things even easier, the reins convert into a leadrope – how amazing is that? ❯❯

> I was pretty blown away by Tizzy's top speed!

Endurance rides

Competitive endurance rides vary from 16–160km so it's really easy for anyone to get into. If your pony is in regular work, he'll almost certainly be fit enough for a 16km ride. But endurance isn't just about riding for miles and miles in the countryside – there's lots of planning and horse care involved, too. Before you even cross the start line, you'll need to pass a vet inspection. Those who are cleared to ride will then proceed onto the course and there's a final vet inspection at the end. Each rider has a crew to help keep their horses in top condition throughout the ride and on rides over 40km there are vet checks during the race.

Vet inspection

Passing vet inspections is the most important part of endurance riding. The horse's welfare always comes first, so even if a rider's first across the finish line, they won't win if their horse isn't in tip top condition. There are a number of different ways the vet will check your pony to see if he's in good shape...

- ### HEART RATE
To be able to compete, the horse's resting heart rate must be below 64 beats per minute (bpm). The heart rate can be measured using a stethoscope and counting the number of beats over a one-minute period. Monitoring the heart rate is normally the first test a vet will perform, in case the horse becomes stressed by the other elements of the vetting process – causing his heart rate to increase

- ### MUCUS MEMBRANE
These special tissues can tell us lots about how the heart is functioning and whether blood is pumping around the horse's body as it should be. The mucus membrane is found where the skin meets an orifice, such as the mouth, nostrils and conjunctival sac in the eyes, and should be pink and moist. Any changes to its appearance could indicate a lack of oxygenated blood around the body so the vet will check each horse's gums and pull back the eyelid to reveal the conjunctival sac

- ### PINCH TEST
This simple test for dehydration is easy and effective – and you can do it yourself. Standing by the horse's shoulder, the vet will pinch the skin on his neck and see how quickly it returns to its original position. If it takes over two seconds to return to shape, it's a sign that the horse is dehydrated

- ### BODY CONDITION
The vet will check each horse over for lumps and bumps and will also feel his muscles to make sure they aren't really tight – which can be an indication of azoturia, a muscle cramp that causes stiffness and pain

- ### TROT UP
The final element of the vetting is the trot up. Each rider will be asked to trot away from the vet for 30 metres, turn a circle with the handler on the outside so they don't block the vet's view, and then trot the horse back. If the horse shows any signs of lameness he'll fail the vetting

Fit to ride

Most endurance riders will do interval training with their horses, which means they do circuits at varying speeds, and look at how quickly their horse recovers. They'll often ride faster in training than in a real race so that the horse's heart gets used to working hard and will find the demands of a race relatively easy. When we were training we hit an incredible top speed of 41.8km per hour!

Did you know?
Your time doesn't stop when you cross the line – it keeps ticking until your horse is fully recovered and completes his vet checks.

Team work

Endurance riders always have a great crew behind them to help look after their horses. They'll be out on course at designated checkpoints with water bottles for sloshing all over the horses to keep them cool. On long rides, the crew will even have food for the horses to eat during the race.

The crew are absolutely vital at the end of an endurance race, too. It's their quick thinking, great horse care and monitoring that lets the rider know when the horse is recovered sufficiently to head to the vet inspection and hopefully stop the clock!

CASPER'S
WARDROBE

I often feel like the boys have a bigger wardrobe than I do, but as I want them to be as happy as possible, it's important they have the right kit, too

PERFECT PJS

On chilly evenings and especially during the winter months when Casper is clipped, I use a stable rug to stop him from feeling the cold. Casper's a really good doer, so rugs with 200g fill are usually enough for him. Opting for a rug that has a mane and tail flap, like this one, stops any drafts and are particularly useful when I've clipped his neck hair.

COME RAIN OR SHINE

In winter, all the horses wear a mediumweight turnout rug to keep them warm and dry. I look for rugs that are waterproof, breathable and have a ripstop fabric. My favourite winter rugs have a full neck and a tail flap as it helps to keep the horses clean. In the spring I often use a no-fill rug like this one to keep Casper dry – especially if I plan to ride him that day. No-fill rugs are perfect for keeping the horses dry, without making them too warm.

BUZZ OFF

Flies can really annoy horses in the summer, but there are lots of things you can do to prevent them becoming a nuisance. Fly repellents can be a big help, or you can use a rug and fly mask for protection. This zebra print isn't just Casper's latest fashion statement, the black and white stripes actually confuse the flies so they don't know where to land, which makes this rug even more effective! I use a full mask on Casper, but you can also get ones without ears, ones with a hole for the forelock to poke through, and others stop just below the cheekbones leaving the nose exposed.

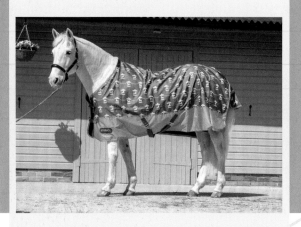

TRAVEL READY

When Casper's off on an adventure in the van, the most important things are his comfort and safety. I like to use travel boots for him that fasten with Velcro tabs and have a tough reinforced section around the pastern area. They cover his legs from just above the hock and knee right down to his coronet band. I also use a tail guard that protects his tail from being rubbed. This one wraps around his tail and fastens with Velcro. You could also use a tail bandage if you wanted to.

I always use a leather headcollar whenever I travel the horses just in case they need to get free in an emergency – as leather will break much more easily than some man-made materials. Most of the year, Casper wears a light breathable sheet to travel in as he can get quite warm on the lorry and this wicks the moisture away from him so that he doesn't get sweaty.

JUMP TO IT

Casper's favourite thing in the world to do is jump, but it's really important that he's super-comfy in his tack and that he's got the protection he needs. I'm very lucky that Casper can be jumped in the same bridle he uses for everything else, with a rubber snaffle bit and a plain cavesson noseband. He wears a five-point breastplate to make sure his saddle doesn't slip backwards and when we're jumping on grass he wears a stud girth to make sure he doesn't injure himself when he really picks up his front feet over a fence. I have a forward cut jump saddle as it helps to keep me in the perfect position over a fence, too.

Casper wears tendon boots on his front legs to protect him from injury if he were to strike into them with his hinds. On his back legs, he wears fetlock boots to protect him from brushing injuries.

DRESSAGE DIVA

I don't often use white saddle pads as it can make grey horses look really yellow, but it does look super-smart for dressage. Casper has a dressage saddle, which has longer flaps than his jump saddle and supports my leg in a longer position. His plain bridle and snaffle bit are both dressage legal – so we use the same kit for dressage and jumping. While you can't use any boots or bandages on your pony's legs for competition, I do like to warm up with a set of dressage wraps or brushing boots on to prevent any injuries.

JUMP TO IT

Find your jumping groove with my go-to grids!

WHY GRIDS?

Whenever I have an issue with my jumping, my absolute go-to is gridwork. There's a grid to solve every problem and they're fun for you and your pony, too. Jumping through a grid creates a safe zone for you to slowly build on your skills and overcome any problems you've been having. If you set up your grid correctly, all the striding is done for you. This moves the emphasis from jumping, to simply getting to the first pole. Once your pony's gone over that pole, concentrate on riding straight and forwards. Then, let your pony – and the grid – do all the hard work for you!

LET'S GET STARTED

Grids may look small compared to some of the fences you might jump while you're out competing, but they can be hard work for your pony – so it's as important as ever to warm up properly. I like to give Casper a walk around the arena, making sure he's marching on and taking me forward. I use this time to settle him and give him a really good look at all the jumps and obstacles in the arena. If there are banners waving about in the breeze, I always make sure Casper sees these on both reins, too. Once he's settled it's time to pick up trot. I use a half-halt so Casper knows I'm about to ask something of him and then nudge him into trot. Right from the start, I'm looking to see if he responds to my leg aid immediately or if he's not quite switched on yet. I like to ride some trot, walk, trot transitions to make sure I've got his attention.

Next it's time to move up a gear and have a canter. I usually ask Casper to go forward in canter, and then collect for a few strides so I know he's listening and that I've got the adjustable canter I need for jumping. Depending on his mood, I find that Casper can respond differently to me, so I have a plan for 'Spicy Casper' and a plan for 'Potato Casper' – who might need waking up a bit! ❯❯

GRIDS AREN'T JUST FOR JUMPING

Whenever I build a grid, I like to make the most of it by riding in and out of the different elements. If you're able to build your grid in the centre of the school, you can ride serpentines through the spaces in between the fences, or ride circles around the end poles. It's a real test of accuracy, and if you're feeling super-confident why not try riding walk trot or trot canter transitions as you weave your way in and out of the grid?

THE SET-UP

Place a pole 3m in front of a cross pole and another 3m after the cross pole.

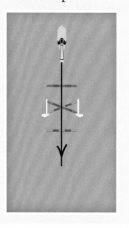

WHOA THERE SPICY CASPER!

This simple three-part grid is great for slowing horses who have a tendency to rush. By placing a pole a stride before the fence and a pole one stride after the fence, I'm giving Casper something to look at and focus his attention on – rather than hurtling towards the fence.

HOW TO RIDE IT:

I pick up a forward canter and head towards the centre of the first pole, making sure that Casper's listening to me and that we're straight as we come off the corner. I keep my leg on and allow slightly with my hands as I go over the pole. Having a pole before the fence should put Casper on a good stride for the cross pole element, so I keep riding positively and fold through my hips as he jumps. The final pole is just one stride from landing, so I keep looking ahead and allow with my hands as we go over this final element, which is really helpful for making sure Casper doesn't race off.

THE SET-UP

Start with one cross pole followed by two poles 3-3.6m apart. Have extra sets of wings and poles ready for you to create a second and third cross pole once your pony has jumped through the grid.

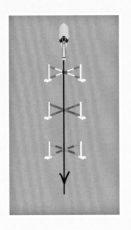

TOP TECHNIQUE

Jumping bounce fences teaches horses to be nimble on their feet and improve their jumping technique. Because it's a gymnastic exercise, Casper will be working really hard – so it's important to keep the fences small and not ride through the grid too many times.

HOW TO RIDE IT:

I approach the centre of the cross pole, then fold from my hips and allow with my hands as Casper jumps the first element. I try to keep him straight as he continues over the next two poles. When we both feel confident doing this, I make the second element another small cross pole. Approaching the grid again in canter, I make sure Casper's going forward without getting too fast. As he lands from the first element, he needs to take off for the second straight away – with no stride in between. I fold slightly forward for each element as Casper takes off, and keep my hands soft.

When we're bouncing through elements one and two no problem, it's time to add a third – where the last pole is. When I approach this time, I don't need to be going any faster – a forward and bouncy canter is perfect. I try to make sure I stay soft with my hands as Casper jumps parts 1–3, all without taking a stride in between.

This Esme

Running free

Want to know who's the boss of our herd? I'll give you a clue, it's not me!

WILD THINGS

The herd dynamic of horses living in the wild is slightly different to the herds we know with our smaller fenced off paddocks. Each herd has a lead stallion and a lead mare who will have earned their place at the top. Guiding the rest of the herd from the front, the lead mare keeps the horses moving towards food and water and makes sure they stay safe. The lead stallion controls the herd from behind – ensuring there aren't any stragglers, and warding off predators. Luckily for Mickey, Casper and Joey, there aren't many predators in England and they have food and water literally on tap!

WHERE DO I FIT IN?

You might be surprised to know that horses don't consider their humans to be part of the herd. For starters we're predators – so even though I'm vegetarian they have a very different relationship with me. In fact, some experts say that horses' relationships with humans are based entirely on their experience with people through their life. You might find that the most gentle and caring pony is a dominant force to be reckoned with in the field, or a tricky pony is actually bottom of the pack.

RESOURCES FOR HORSES

There are only a few things horses really need to be happy in life – food and water being the most important. If you want to know which horse is the most dominant in your herd, you'll need to watch them eating and drinking. The one who's in charge will have his pick of both. In my little herd, Joey is 100% the boss. When I need to put hay out in the field in winter, Joey always gets to choose which haynet he's having before the others do.

THE BATTLE FOR LAST PLACE

It's so interesting to see the horses' different personalities in action. Casper can be quite a worrier and as a result he seems to have gladly handed over his top dog status to Joey. In his eyes, having second pick of the haynets is a fair swap for not having the responsibility for the safety of the herd. Mickey on the other hand will always try to sneak up the ranks. He's forever on the lookout for an opportunity to move off the bottom spot.

BEST PALS

Within the herd, horses often form one special bond with another horse. They're likely to be their favourite grooming partner and the horse they spend the most time with. As my herd is so small, you'll often find different combinations of Casper, Mickey and Joey grooming each other – Joey in particular loves a really good scratch.

TIME FOR ZZZZ

Being part of a herd is so important for a horse's ability to sleep. Within the herd they'll take turns to watch for any dangers while the others get some Zzzzs.

This Esme

Having second pick of the haynets is a fair swap for not having responsibility

A SPRING IN
YOUR STEP

If you're anything like me, you probably spend more time in trot than in any other pace. But what do you really know about it? Here's my colour-coded guide to trot

TO THE BEAT

Trot is a two-beat gait where the horse's legs move in diagonal pairs.

UP AND DOWN

You can choose to rise to the trot or go sitting. Most people opt to rise, unless they're training for dressage. It's best to warm up your pony in rising trot because it allows him to swing through his back and warm up his muscles.

To rise to the trot, you lift your hips forward and up before gently sitting back down for each stride. When you're starting out, your instructor might call this your up-downs as it can help to call *up, down, up, down* as you go until you get the hang of it. When you ride around the arena you should sit when your horse's outside shoulder is back – this is called being on the correct diagonal. Each time you change the rein in trot, ride a double sit so that you change your diagonal, too.

Did you know?
There are four different types of trot – working, medium, collected and extended. Plus the advanced movements of piaffe and passage.

Hot to trot

The sequence your horse moves his feet in trot is:

- left hind and right fore together
- right hind and left fore together

In trot there is a moment of suspension – which means all four feet are off the floor at the same time!

WORKING TROT

Your pony's normal trot is what's known as working trot. It should be rhythmical and balanced, with his hind legs clearly tracking up to his front hoof prints.

MEDIUM TROT

As you move up the levels in dressage, the tests will ask you to show a few strides of medium trot. This is the first step towards extended trot and asks your pony to not only take slightly longer steps – but to lengthen a little through his frame as well. He should still be working in an outline, but you need to allow him to lower his head and neck slightly.

EXTENDED TROT

Your pony should cover as much ground as possible in this trot, but his rhythm should be almost exactly the same as all the other types. To master this, your pony will spend more time in the suspension phase of trot – with all four feet off the ground – as he moves forward in a powerful, up hill feeling trot. With Casper, I find the best way to experience extended trot is to ask him to really lengthen his strides as we power up a slight hill out hacking.

COLLECTED TROT

Like extended trot, you don't have to show collected trot in dressage until higher levels. To ride it, you need to ask your pony to shorten his stride and trot with increased elevation. Collected trot isn't about going slowly, it's a more powerful trot where your pony lifts his shoulders and uses his hocks to create a higher and shorter step. Piaffe and passage are both advanced forms of collected trot where the steps get even higher and shorter until you're trotting on the spot!

Ask your pony to really lengthen his strides while you're on a hack

This Esme's
RAD ROUTINES
AUTUMN

I love autumn – the colours are gorgeous and it's still light enough to enjoy a fun hack in the evenings. There's plenty to be done, though, so find out what I get up to at this time of year...

GOOD HAIR DAY

As soon as autumn hits it's time to get the clippers out! The horses get sooo hairy and I have to stay on top of Casper's clip to make sure he doesn't get too hot when I ride him. He loves going for a good canter out on a hack, so it's important to help keep him cool.

STOCKED UP

The equines all come into their stables more often as the weather gets colder, but this means they eat more hay since they aren't eating lots of grass. I always stock up on hay and bedding in the autumn so they have plenty to eat and a comfy bed to sleep on during those cold nights!

RAINY DAYS

My heavier turnout rugs are all super-sparkly clean since I washed them earlier in the year, but it's a great idea to re-proof them, too, which will make sure they're waterproof ready for when the rain comes. I use a spray to apply the waterproofing liquid to my rugs, but you can also paint it on if you prefer.

OUT AND ABOUT

With the evenings getting a bit shorter now, I like to use my favourite short hacking routes that I know I'll have time to complete before it gets dark. If I already have routes in mind, it means I can get out riding ASAP, rather than worrying about where to go.

FIELD FRIENDLY

We have some oak trees surrounding our fields at home, so I have to be super-careful that I pick up any acorns that fall into the horses' fields during the autumn. If any of the equines ate too many of them, it could make them really poorly. Always check for any plants that could hurt your pony, too – I try to keep an eye out for them while I poo-pick the fields.

Add your autumn jobs to my list below...

clipping ☐

clear up acorns ☐

buy bedding and hay ☐

re-proof rugs ☐

plan hacking routes ☐

.... ☐

.... ☐

.... ☐

.... ☐

.... ☐

.... ☐

.... ☐

"I use the shorter hacking routes that I know I'll have time to complete before it gets dark"

AMAZING CUPCAKES

When you've been on the yard all day there's nothing quite like these sweet treats!

What you'll need:

Cakes:
- 1 medium egg
- 60ml vegetable oil
- 125ml semi-skimmed milk
- 125g golden caster sugar
- 200g self-raising flour
- ½ tsp salt

Decoration:
- 160g unsalted butter
- 300g icing sugar, plus a little for dusting
- 1 tbsp milk
- 1 tsp vanilla extract
- green sugar paste
- white sugar paste
- black sugar paste
- coloured sugar paste, to make bridles

Equipment:
- weighing scales
- muffin tray and cases
- 2 large mixing bowls
- electric hand whisk
- sieve
- skewer and oven gloves
- wire cooling rack
- rolling pin
- sharp knife
- palette knife
- small paintbrush

MAKING THE CAKES

1. Preheat the oven to 200°C/180°C fan/Gas 6. Line a muffin tray with paper cases.

2. In a large bowl beat the egg lightly with an electric hand whisk for 1 minute.

3. Add the vegetable oil and the semi-skimmed milk then mix until just combined. Add the golden caster sugar and whisk until you have a smooth batter.

4. Sift in the self-raising flour, add the salt and mix until just smooth. Be careful not to overmix the batter as this will make the cakes tough.

5. Fill the muffin cases two-thirds full and bake for 20–25 minutes, until risen and firm to the touch. To check they are cooked, insert a skewer into the middle and check it comes out clean. Remove from the oven, then leave to cool fully on a wire rack before decorating.

FOR THE DECORATION

1. Mix your buttercream by placing the butter, icing sugar, milk and vanilla extract in the bowl and beat with the electric whisk for 4-5 minutes, or until light and fluffy.

2. Slice the tops off the cakes so that they are level and spread some buttercream on top using a palette knife until you have a smooth surface.

3. Lightly cover the work top with icing sugar. Roll out the green sugar paste and cut out round discs, then place each one on top of a cake.

4. Roll out the white sugar paste and cut out oval shapes, then stick them on the green sugar paste circles using a little water on a paintbrush.

5. Make the ears and stick them to the top (either side) of the oval shape, followed by the eyes and the pony's muzzle and nostrils. Repeat for all the cakes.

6. With some coloured sugar paste, make the bridle by rolling out thin sausage shapes and sticking them to each pony's head with a little water.

7. Finally, create the manes for the ponies by rolling out small thin sausage shapes and layering them on top of the pony's head where its browband is.

Sorry Casper – you're just too tasty!

This Esme

"Why not make all the ponies at your yard and hold a bake sale for charity?"

ROAD RIDER

When it comes to riding on the road, being safe and being seen are the most important things

1. Be safe, be seen

Whenever you head out on the roads, think about how well other road users will be able to see you. The quicker a driver can spot you, the more time they have to react. That could be the difference between them having to slam on the brakes and gently pulling over to let you pass.

It's best to wear a combination of high vis and reflective clothing that can be seen from in front and behind. I've gone for a yellow high vis base layer, which has panels of reflective material sewn into it.

Ideally your pony should also be wearing some high vis – just in case you fall off on a ride. Joey has this high vis bonnet, which not only helps him be seen but also keeps the flies off his ears in summer. During the winter months, I use a high vis exercise sheet with reflective strips on the tail flap.

Try to avoid riding on the roads at night, but if you have to, always wear a light fitted to the right-hand side of your leg or arm, showing a white light at the front and a red light behind.

Don't forget your safety helmet! In the UK children under 14 years of age are required to wear an up to standard riding helmet – but it's good practice for everyone.

2. Are you road ready?

There are a lot of different things for your pony to look at on the road, so it's really important you're confident he will move off your leg if you ask him to – and that you're in control. You can practise this in the arena at home. Ride lots of transitions and each time ask yourself *was my pony really listening to me?* Test yourself by giving your pony something to look at that he might encounter while you're out on the road – for example, a wheelie bin. What are his reactions like? It's OK for your pony to look at something new, but you want him to trust you and move forward when you ask him to. »

> *It's up to you to communicate with other road users so they know where you're going*

3. It's a sign

Horses and ponies aren't fitted with indicators and brake lights like cars are, so it's up to you to communicate to other road users so they know where you're going. Here are the most common rider signals...

- If you're turning right, look over your right shoulder to see if anything's coming, signal with your right arm held at 90° to your body and the palm of your hand facing forward. Check to see if the way ahead is safe, look over your right shoulder again for any traffic and then turn to the right if all is clear.
- To turn left, look over your right shoulder to see if any vehicles are coming. Use your left arm to signal left by holding it at 90° to your body with your palm facing forward. Check behind you once more by looking over your right shoulder. If the way is ahead is safe, make your turn.
- To ask other road users to slow down, hold your right arm out at 90° but this time your palm should face down to the floor. Now raise and lower your arm four or five times to tell other road users you want them to slow down.
- If a car stops or slows down for you, thank them by raising a hand, or with a smile and an exaggerated nod if it's not safe to take a hand off the reins.

4. Two's company

If you or your pony are new to riding on the road, it's important to go out with an experienced horse or pony. In the UK, you can ride two abreast unless you're riding on narrow or busy roads when you should ride in single file. Position the horse with the least experience of riding on the road on the inside so that they are away from passing cars, and if you need to ride in single file always put the more experienced horse in front.

Always keep to the left!

5. Pole position

When you head out on the road, it's really important to follow the rules to avoid accidents. Always stay to the left hand side of the road – just like cars do. It's best to avoid roundabouts if you can, but if you do have to navigate one, keep left and indicate right if you do not intend to leave the roundabout at the exit you are passing. Signal left before you leave the roundabout and keep a look out for vehicles crossing your path. You must not ride on footpaths or pavements.

When you find that special horse
who you want to gallop on to the
end of the world and back!

DAY IN THE LIFE OF THE DONKEYS

Find out what my other four-legged friends get up to each day

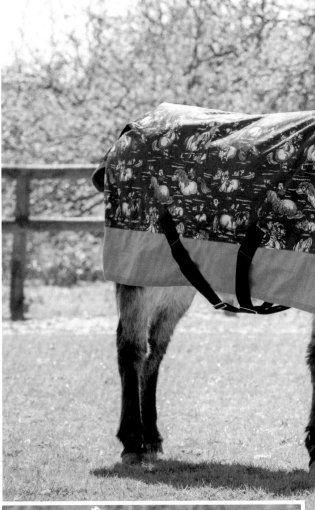

Mmm breakfast

The donkeys have a bucket feed after I've had my breakfast. They don't eat as early as the ponies or they'd wake up the whole village with their braying each morning. I make sure Willow has hers somewhere quiet, so the boys don't try to steal it!

Hoof it

I pick out their hooves every day just as I do with the horses. This makes sure their feet stay in tip top condition and gives me a chance to check their overall health and look for anything that's wrong.

H20

For most of the year, the donkeys are free to roam in and out of their field shelter and paddock so they always have access to their water trough. But just because I don't need to fill it every day, doesn't mean I don't need to check it. I have a quick look to make sure the water's okay every day and give the trough a proper clean out whenever it needs it.

Cute cuddles

A day on the yard wouldn't be the same without some cuddles from the donkeys. Willow and I have a special bond – but Bruno and Toby also love a good scratch and a hug.

Just chilling

Donkeys are really social animals and often form pair bonds that can last a lifetime. Bruno and Toby are especially close and do everything together – whether that's going for a drink, eating grass or watching me ride in the arena, they just love each other!

Poo patrol

I'm quite a perfectionist when it comes to having nice clean paddocks, so I try to poo pick the fields every day. It's not just for show – clearing the droppings from their fields protects horses and donkeys from having an excessive worm burden.

Waterproofs on

Donkeys don't have the same oils in their coats as horses do, so it's really important they always have enough shelter from the rain. My donkeys also have little turnout rugs for when the weather's bad and fly rugs for the summer, too!

Tea time

I normally feed the donkeys their dinner around 6pm each evening. They love tucking in to their hard feed, which is a good job as I have to sneak some medicine into Willow's now that she's getting a bit older. They just have a small amount of fibre-based feed so that they don't become overweight.

FULL SPEED AHEAD

Cantering your pony is probably one of the most exhilarating things you can do – especially when you're having a blast across the countryside or on the beach!

TO THE BEAT
Canter is a three-beat gait

THE RIGHT LEAD
Depending on which direction your pony's travelling in canter, the order of his footfalls will vary – this is known as the canter lead. If you're moving in a clockwise direction, your pony needs to be on the right lead – this means his footfalls will be left hind, right hind and left foreleg as a diagonal pair, followed by the right foreleg. If you're moving in an anti-clockwise direction your pony should be on the left lead – which is right hind, left hind and right foreleg as a pair and finally the left foreleg.

Did you know?
To ask a pony to canter, press your outside leg behind the girth and your inside leg on the girth. This is because the outside hind takes the first canter step, so you should focus on asking that leg step into canter by using your outside leg aid.

Step to it

When you think about your pony's footfalls, canter is much more complicated than walk or trot. The sequence is:
- outside hind
- inside hind leg and outside foreleg moving as a diagonal pair
- inside foreleg

Canter has a moment of suspension when all four feet are off the ground at the same time.

WORKING CANTER

Just like with trot, working canter is the name given to your pony's normal canter at the lower levels of dressage. He should work in an outline and move forward in a rhythmical and energetic canter.

COLLECTED CANTER

While collected canter asks for shorter steps than a normal working canter, it also requires more power. Your pony needs to engage his hind quarters to lift his front end. He should maintain the rhythm, but shorten his whole frame and take elevated, even steps. Top level riders use collected canter to perform Grand Prix movements, such as pirouettes.

MEDIUM AND EXTENDED CANTER

In dressage, medium canter is the first step between working canter and extended canter. To ride medium canter you'll need to ask your pony to extend his frame slightly and take longer strides without changing his rhythm. Extended canter isn't asked for until higher levels of dressage but, to do it, the horse needs to cover as much ground as possible, while maintaining his rhythm and outline.

Did you know?

Gallop isn't just a fast canter – the footfalls are different. Just like canter, there are left and right leads of gallop but, instead of moving as a diagonal pair, all four feet hit the ground at separate times, making gallop a four-beat gait.

Did you know?

The average speed of a canter is 10–17mph.

THE LONG AND SHORT OF IT

Perfecting your pony's paces is super-useful for when you're jumping, too. It's important to learn how to shorten and lengthen your pony's strides so his canter becomes really adjustable. That way, you'll be able to find the right stride to a fence much more easily.

t's fair to say that mounted games is not an entirely new sport for me. Back in my Pony Club days, Mickey and I did a lot of gymkhanas and mounted games together. We had loads of fun and although we weren't exactly the speediest of competitors, sometimes slow and steady would win the race. Keen to find out how the top riders train for mounted games, I met with World and European Team Champion, and Reserve World Individual Champion, Sadie Lock.

The history of mounted games

HRH Prince Philip devised mounted games as a fun team competition for young riders who didn't have expensive show ponies. The sport involves a series of races where teams of four or five riders compete against each other at speed while tackling tight turns and tests of skill.

The first mounted games championship was held at Horse of the Year Show back in 1957, where the winning team were awarded the Prince Philip Cup. The Pony Club still organises the Prince Philip Cup and you can go and cheer on your favourite teams in the final at Horse of the Year Show.

The popularity of the Pony Club mounted games grew and grew, however, riders had to stop when they reached the age of 14. To combat this, a man named Norman Patrick established The Mounted Games Association of Great Britain (MGAGB) in the 1980s, which allowed riders to continue competing for as long as they wanted to. »

What to look for in a mounted games pony

The most important thing to look for is the right temperament. There's lots of different equipment used in mounted games, and riders often find themselves galloping their ponies with swords, flags and other bits and pieces that can seem pretty scary – so it's important you find a pony who's brave and stays calm under pressure. For MGAGB events, there's a maximum height of 15hh for horses and ponies. Other than that, any pony can take part in games, but to compete at the top level you'll need a pony who is quick, agile and really responsive to you.

Skills practice

Before taking part in any games, there are some simple skills you can try on your own. Have a go at riding with just one hand. In mounted games you'll need to use your free hand to pick up objects, pass a baton to your team mates or maybe even use a sword to collect hoops! Start slowly in walk, then build up to trot and even canter when you think you're ready.

Being able to accelerate and decelerate quickly is another important skill for games. To practise this, set up a cone at each end of your arena and see if you can start at one cone, work your way up through the paces to canter before stopping at the second one. To begin with, you might only get to a trot before you need to start slowing down again – but keep practising as the top riders perform a halt to canter from the start line and stop at the other end in just a fraction of a second.

Tight turns can be the difference between winning and losing – so this is another important skill to master with your pony. Again, start slowly and work your way up the gears until you can turn neatly round a pole in trot or canter. This kind of training will be demanding on your pony at first, so just try a few tight turns each time you ride until they're used to it.

A leap of faith

Top games riders vault onto their ponies at the gallop to save precious seconds. It's best to get the hang of the vaulting action on something like a gymnastics horse that won't go anywhere before you practise on the real thing though! Once you're feeling confident with the gym horse, you can have a go with the real thing. Ask someone to hold your pony still for you to begin with, then hold the saddle and make little jumps so that your pony gets used to it. If he's not bothered by this, have a go at vaulting straight into the saddle from the ground. If you want to challenge yourself, you can ask your friend to lead your pony as you run alongside – then leap up into the saddle. Before long you'll be vaulting on in gallop just like the pros!

My favourite mounted games races:

BENDING RACE

This is a fast and furious dash from one end to the other while weaving in and out of the poles. When you reach the end of the line of poles, ride a tight turn around the last one before weaving your way back to the finish as fast as you can. In a team game, you then pass a baton to the next rider who completes the same course.

Try it at home by putting five cones along the centre line and start by trotting in and out of them. Your pony will need to listen to your leg and rein aids so that he knows which side of each cone to go. Once you've mastered it in trot, why not step it up a gear and try a canter?

FLAG RACE

You'll need five flags and two holders for this game. Place one holder halfway down the arena with four flags in it and the other close to the end. In the team race, the first rider sets off holding a flag and rides all the way to the end, placing their flag into the holder as they turn around and head back – stopping to collect another flag as they pass the middle cone. They then pass their flag to the next rider, who does the same thing. Riders three and four repeat this until all the flags are in the far holder and the last rider crosses the line carrying a flag.

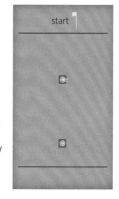

SWORD RACE

This game is super-fun, but it does require specialist equipment so it's not easy to try at home. You need four bending poles – each with a sword ring – and a sword. Set up the poles 7–9m apart along the length of the arena. The first rider sets off and collects the first ring on their sword then completes the course before handing the sword to rider number two, who's waiting at the opposite end. The second rider collects another ring and hands the sword to rider number three. The third rider does the same before handing over to rider number four who collects the final ring and crosses the finish line.

MUG RACE

To set up this game, you'll need four poles and two metal or plastic mugs. Put the poles in a straight line and place a mug on the first and third pole. On your pony, collect the mug from the first pole and place it on the second. Then, pick up the mug from the third pole and place it on the fourth before crossing the line. In a team game, the second rider sets off from the opposite end. They pick up the mug from the first pole they pass and put it on the next, then collect a mug from the third pole they get to before putting it on the final one and crossing the line. The third rider repeats the same course as the first, and the fourth rider follows the same pattern as the second. This game's a lot harder than it looks – it takes a lot of skill to replace the mugs at speed!

THINK POSITIVE

Follow my tips on how to improve your mindset

Just for fun

It's great to be mega-focused on improving your riding, but sometimes it can be just as beneficial to take the pressure off. Never forget that you ride because you love it, not just to win red rosettes! So, schedule in time to go for a fun, relaxed hack with friends or play gymkhana games in the school. Not only will it help you remember that you don't have to be serious all the time, your pony's sure to enjoy it, too.

When you're working with your fave pony, it's super-important that you stay positive – even when things don't go to plan! So, to help you, I've got some tips on how you can get into the ideal headspace for success.

Remember, remember

It's really easy to focus on the goals you have yet to achieve, and forget about all the amazing things you've done already. If your goals feel like they're a long way off, it's a good idea to have a look back through old videos and photos of your riding, and remember how far you've come! Even though it's great to have dreams, never forget that you're awesome already.

Top tip

Why not keep a riding journal noting all the lessons and comps you do? Then you can look through it when you need a boost.

Get into the ideal headspace!

Thank your lucky stars each day

Even if you're not riding at the level you want quite yet, or don't have your own pony, transport or fancy arena, make sure you sit back and appreciate what you do have! If you're grateful for all the awesome opportunities that come your way, you'll be much happier than if you compare yourself to others all the time.

Top tip

At the end of each day, try listing three things you're grateful for. It could be that you had an awesome lesson, epic hack or that your fave pony gave you a lovely cuddle!

Give yourself time to think

Good company

It's a lot easier to be positive when the people around you are, too! Do your friends help encourage you and let you know when you've done well? Do you feel super-motivated after you've had a riding lesson? Have a think about who in your life helps lift you up – your friends, instructor or parents – and spend as much time around them as possible!

Best bits

When you've had a lesson or comp, instead of dwelling on what didn't go so well, focus on the highlights! Didn't get the dressage score you'd hoped for? Well, if your pony behaved himself and did some great circles and lines, then fab! Knocked a pole showjumping but popped a scary filler first time? Amazing! If you celebrate your small wins, you'll be set to improve on what went wrong so you can do even better next time.

Streeeeeetch
IT OUT

We all feel better after we've had a good stretch, and when there are treats involved Joey can't see what's not to love about having a good workout!

SUPER STRETCHES

Just like humans, our equines' athletic performance can be improved by having a good stretch. Using treats to incentivise natural movements of the horse can reduce tension and stiffness, and improve suppleness and flexibility. I've been using carrot stretches with Joey for a few months now and his range of movement's definitely improving. I'm pretty sure he thinks they're 10/10, too!

Top tip

If you've any concerns about your pony always speak to a vet first.

STRETCH 1
NECK STRETCH ACROSS THE FRONT LEGS

To ask Joey to get into this stretch I need to position myself beside his foreleg on the side I want him to bend towards. Using a carrot or treat, I bring his head down and to the side of his fetlock before asking him to hold the stretch for 5–10 seconds. Then I reward him with the treat. For sideways stretches like this one it's really important Joey does them the same number of times in each direction.

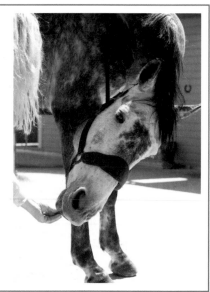

STRETCH 2
THROUGH THE LEGS

This stretch works on Joey's back, neck and abdominal muscles. Using the treat as an incentive, I ask Joey to stretch his head down towards his front legs as far as he can manage. I try to make sure he does this in one gradual movement by keeping the treat within reach so that he doesn't snatch his head. Once Joey reaches the end of his natural movement, I hold the stretch for 5–10 seconds before rewarding him with the treat. Ideally, I'd like Joey to reach down towards the floor a little more than he is – but he's still learning this stretch.

Top tip

If your pony's greedy, you can use a low-calorie lick instead of a carrot or treats.

STRETCH 3
TO THE POINT OF HIP

This time I'm using the treat to guide Joey's nose towards the point of his hip. When I get a really good stretch, I hold it for a few seconds and then reward him with a treat. This stretch works on the muscles between his ribs on the opposite side to the way he's stretching as well as his shoulder and neck – so again, I always need to repeat it on both sides.

Top tip

Hold each stretch for 5–10 seconds before you give your pony the reward.

Top tip

For the best results you'll need to perform these stretches at least a couple of times each week.

83

ESME'S SHOW GUIDE:

YOUR FIRST HUNTER TRIAL

*Everyone loves a cross-country sesh,
but are you ready to take it to competition?*

Joey and I competed in our first ever hunter trial together in late 2020 and it's an experience I'll never forget for all the right reasons. Even though it was somewhere new, there were horses everywhere and lots of new sights and sounds for him, we made it from the start box to the end of the course at our own pace and tackled some challenging jumps along the way. I was unbelievably proud!

Although I'd done lots of schooling, I'd never actually competed in cross-country as Casper's quite nervous and doesn't like to go to shows. Since Joey's competition, though, I've been itching to get out and do more, not only to build on our experience but also because it was heaps of fun! Here are my top tips on making sure you're as prepared as you can be.

> *It was an experience I'll never forget – for all the right reasons!*

SCHOOLING SAVVY

You definitely don't want to turn up to a hunter trial without having jumped cross-country fences before – it would be like sitting an exam you've not revised for! Going to a cross-country course or booking a lesson with your instructor before you go is a massive advantage. I took Joey to a course before my competition and practised...

- **different and spooky fences** You can expect to find steps, skinnies, ditches and water jumps in a hunter trial, so you definitely want to make sure your pony is familiar and confident with them before show day. Approach new fences in trot first. I always like to give Joey a long rein to investigate the water so he knows it won't hurt him
- **technical stuff** Hunter trials often involve twists and turns between fences, so be sure your pony is taking combinations and more complicated lines in his stride before you head to a competition
- **speed control** While you want to get out of the saddle for a faster canter in a forward seat between fences – which means you'll be standing slightly in your stirrups – when it comes to trickier jumps, your pony will need to slow down into more of a showjumping canter, so practise switching between the two. It's also a good test of your pony's brakes!

PHENOMENAL FITNESS

One thing I discovered at our competition is that Joey's stamina is really important – I felt him start to get tired towards the end of the course and we lost our rhythm. It dawned on me that when I school him, I usually jump a couple of fences then give him a rest. Since then, I always make sure we jump a number of cross-country fences with plenty of canter work in between, and his fitness has got so much better! We also do loads of hacking up hills, which helps a lot.

Kit list

As well as all my regular kit, here's what I take with me to a hunter trial...

- **stud girth** I like to use a stud girth for jumping – it helps protect your pony's tummy when he snaps up his front legs over a fence, especially if he's wearing...
- **studs** These are perfect for helping your pony out on slippy ground. I always keep them with my stud kit, which has everything I'll need to unpack, clean and plug the stud holes in Joey's shoes, as well as screw them in
- **cross-country and overreach boots** To help protect Joey's legs, I use special boots that are tough yet flexible and well-ventilated to keep him cool and allow water to drain out. Overreach boots cover his front hooves, so if he reaches too far with his back ones he can't clip his heels and hurt himself
- **body protector** It's essential to wear a body protector for cross-country – you won't be allowed to compete if you forget it. Always make sure it's up to the current safety standard and fits properly. I also like to use an air jacket, which inflates to protect me should I fall off
- **medical armband** This fits around the top of your arm and contains all your medical information just in case. It's another cross-country necessity – ask your parents to help you fill it in

Top tip

Your pony could be very hot and thirsty after a long cross-country course so make sure you take plenty of water with you.

››

MATCHY-MATCHY MAYHEM

While in dressage and showjumping it's considered correct to use plain saddlecloths and smart jackets, competing in a hunter trial is the time to let your best matchy-matchy set shine! There's no limit to the colours you can show off as you gallop round the course, so let your imagination run wild!

Top tip

Speak to your instructor about any tack changes – it might be that they recommend you try a different bit or a martingale.

ON THE DAY

Things will feel quite a bit different on a competition day versus a schooling session – here's what I learnt…

- **watch the clock** Everything seems to take longer on show day, so pack as much of your stuff as you can the night before and leave plenty of time for getting there
- **big atmosphere** Hunter trial venues are often vast and busy. Be prepared to give your pony time to look around and settle before you get on
- **hold his hand** Your pony might not be quite as settled as he is in a schooling venue, so be prepared to encourage him with your voice and use your leg aids
- **go with your gut** I listened to Joey the whole way round the course, and ended up skipping out a couple of fences I didn't think he was ready to jump. This took the pressure off us both and I'm so pleased I did. Fortunately, I was at a really friendly venue that let me continue around the course, but you may find officials ask you to retire and leave the course if you miss a jump. All that really matters is that you come away having had a fun and enjoyable experience with your pony!

Did you know?
Cross-country fences have coloured flags either side that tell you which direction to jump it in – the red should always be on your right.

Top tip

Give your pony an extra-long cool-down and keep him walking until he's got his breath back – whether you're riding or leading him.

Did you know?
If you don't have your own number bib you'll have to borrow one from the secretary on the day. Don't forget to hand it back in when you've finished!

POSITIVE VIBES ONLY

Want to know something? My first hunter trial with Joey was technically a fail, because we were eliminated for missing out jumps. But I don't see it that way at all. He exceeded all my expectations by being so well behaved and trying his best. He was a bit spooky and threw some interesting shapes, but I learnt so much about how we could improve next time round, too.

So often riders get bogged down with the things that didn't go well and forget that, overall, they had a fantastic experience and made real progress. In everything I do, I dwell on the things that went well and take lessons from what didn't quite go to plan so I can improve next time. Allow yourself to revel in the good times and your competition day will be all the sweeter for it!

MAKING A
difference

*Using my voice to raise awareness of
this incredible charity*

Back in 2019 I became an ambassador for Brooke. The charity works with owners, governments and local policy makers to make sustainable improvements for the lives of working animals and the people who depend on them. Working livestock are essential to the livelihoods of millions of people across the globe, but all too often the welfare of these animals isn't protected. Brooke's policy of education and knowledge sharing helps owners see that better care will improve the ability of the horse, donkey or mule to carry out tasks like pulling carts or carrying heavy loads. When working animals are fit and well, the role they do can reduce poverty and support essential access to water for families across low and middle income countries.

I was lucky enough to see Brooke's work in Senegal first hand and see the huge difference that donations make to the lives of working equines and the people who depend on them. Brooke's focus on working with the community to create lifelong change is truly inspiring. By training farriers to look after horses' and donkeys' feet properly, the working animals will be more comfortable and able to work – which helps the community, too. Once a farrier is fully trained, Brooke will work with them to help train other farriers so that the knowledge is shared and more and more animals can benefit from good hoof care.

Working with the community doesn't stop there. Brooke took on a huge challenge when working out what to do with all the waste working equines produce. The solution they came up with was a school powered by poo! That's right, poo power converts the 8–10 piles each equine creates every day into biogas, which can be used for cooking, or to create electricity to power lighting once the dung's processed in the right way. The best bit is that it also benefits equines by preventing build-up of dung, which is bad for their hooves and can create a heavy worm burden, too. All the poo is collected and processed at the school using simple hand-powered machinery. The school gets free fuel and the remaining poo is used as fertiliser on the fields. It's a win, win, win response to a stinky situation!

MY HACKATHON

You can get involved with raising money for Brooke by taking part in My Hackathon. Casper and I took the challenge last year and had a fantastic time exploring countryside we hadn't seen before to get our miles up. This time, you can choose 50, 100 or 250 miles as your goal and take as long as you need to complete it. Why not see if any other riders from your yard would like to join you or ride with a friend like I did with Natasha Baker – don't forget to ask for sponsorship, too!

Tea party

If you don't ride or have regular access to a horse or pony, why not hold a tea party instead? I hosted one for Mickey, Casper and special guest, Harry, which you can see over on Brooke's YouTube channel, but you could use my cupcake recipe on page 64 and invite humans instead. Get your friends and family involved, have a super afternoon and raise some money for a great cause at the same time!

This Esme's
RAD ROUTINES
WINTER

Winter might not be my fave time of the year, but there's still plenty to love about caring for horses through the colder months – and plenty to do for them, too. Here's what I get up to...

LIGHT THE WAY

We have some lights around our stables, but starting at 6am means giving the equines their breakfast in the dark. So, I make sure I have plenty of torches fully charged and by the door, ready for when the clocks change.

HEAD INDOORS

I might not do quite so much with the horses during winter, but it's still super-fun to get out and about. I like to check out the local indoor venues and find out what clinics and shows they're running through the winter. That way, I can keep practising and having loads of fun even when the weather's bad.

HACK TO IT

I still love to squeeze in as many hacks as possible, but it's mega-important that I have plenty of high-vis to keep me, Casper and Joey safe at this time of year. I always wear high-vis to hack, even during the summer, but it's extra-important when visibility can be poor due to bad weather.

SESSION PLANS

It's super-handy to have a few short schooling plans so I can stay focused when I don't have so much time to ride. I like to come up with a couple of 10-minute exercises for each ride, which all work on different things, such as leg-yielding on a spiral or shallow loops in canter.

A QUICK GATE-AWAY

The fields get really muddy at home when it rains, so I have to put up some temporary fencing to stop the equines making the gateways too swampy! I also lay some field mats around them before it gets really wet, which helps protect the ground and the grass so it recovers quicker in spring.

Add your winter jobs to my list below...

preparing torches ☐

check out indoor venues ☐

organise high-vis gear ☐

plan short schooling sessions ☐

gateway maintenance ☐

.... ☐

.... ☐

.... ☐

.... ☐

.... ☐

.... ☐

.... ☐

This Esme

"I like to come up with a couple of 10-minute exercises for each ride"

Make a horseshoe tree dec

Christmas wouldn't be the same without a little memento of the horses on the tree

let's get started

What you'll need:
- horseshoe
- acrylic paint in your choice of colour
- a paint brush
- garden twine or coloured string
- scissors

1

Using your acrylic paint and paint brush, carefully paint the front of the horseshoe. Then, leave it to dry completely.

Top tip

If you don't own a pony, ask your riding school if they could give you a shoe from your favourite pony.

2

Cut a length of twine approximately 1m long. Find the midpoint, then start to wrap it around the shoe from the toe clip as shown. Poke each end under the last wrap of twine to secure it.

3

Take the twine half way up each side of the shoe, then wrap it around a few times and secure as you did before. Aim for the same number of wraps on each side. Finally, tie the two ends together so that you can hang your finished horseshoe on the Christmas tree.

I absolutely love Christmas. These horseshoe decorations are the perfect addition to my tree!

JOUSTING

Hear ye, hear ye! It's time to steppeth into medieval England and discover the wonderful world of jousting – and you don't need to be a knight to give it a try

Ever wanted to take mounted games one step further? Then say hello to jousting. This daredevil sport is centuries old and a test of strength and skill performed by real knights. I was lucky enough to give it a go and I think it was my favourite part of the *Challenge Esme* series. I especially enjoyed taking on the Earl of Warwick in full armour once my training was complete! Think you've got what it takes? Here's everything you need to know.

What is jousting?

Jousts were a popular part of medieval tournaments in which opposing knights would ride at one another along a tilt. Each knight, dressed in armour, would carry a lance that was up to 3m in length and a shield, with the aim being to break the lance on the opponent's shield, or even unseat them! In a challenge à plaisance, hollow lances were used as they'd break more easily. However, in a challenge à la guerre, deadlier weapons were used. Today, jousts and other knightly sports are performed by specially trained stunt riders and horses as part of medieval displays, films, TV and re-enactments, but it's also something anyone can try at an experience day or training centre.

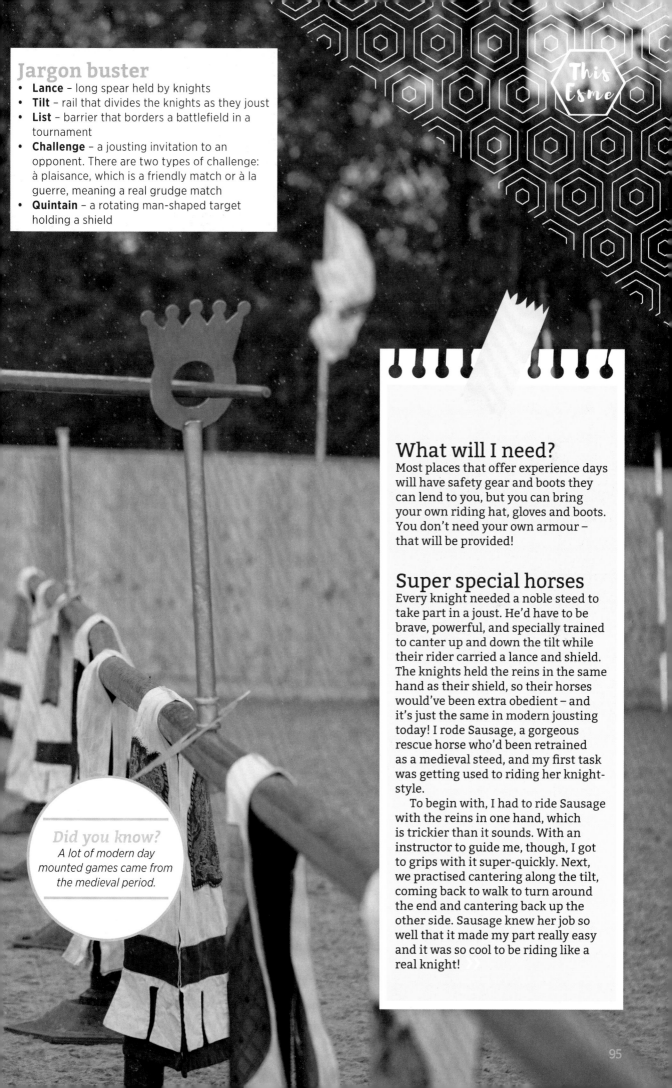

Jargon buster
- **Lance** – long spear held by knights
- **Tilt** – rail that divides the knights as they joust
- **List** – barrier that borders a battlefield in a tournament
- **Challenge** – a jousting invitation to an opponent. There are two types of challenge: à plaisance, which is a friendly match or à la guerre, meaning a real grudge match
- **Quintain** – a rotating man-shaped target holding a shield

Did you know?
A lot of modern day mounted games came from the medieval period.

What will I need?
Most places that offer experience days will have safety gear and boots they can lend to you, but you can bring your own riding hat, gloves and boots. You don't need your own armour – that will be provided!

Super special horses
Every knight needed a noble steed to take part in a joust. He'd have to be brave, powerful, and specially trained to canter up and down the tilt while their rider carried a lance and shield. The knights held the reins in the same hand as their shield, so their horses would've been extra obedient – and it's just the same in modern jousting today! I rode Sausage, a gorgeous rescue horse who'd been retrained as a medieval steed, and my first task was getting used to riding her knight-style.

To begin with, I had to ride Sausage with the reins in one hand, which is trickier than it sounds. With an instructor to guide me, though, I got to grips with it super-quickly. Next, we practised cantering along the tilt, coming back to walk to turn around the end and cantering back up the other side. Sausage knew her job so well that it made my part really easy and it was so cool to be riding like a real knight!

Holding the lance

Once you've got to grips with your noble steed, it's time to pick up your lance and oh my goodness, it's much heavier than you'd expect! Initially, I held the lance in my right hand and balanced the end on my foot to get used to the weight, then I gripped it under my armpit so it was pointing forward ready to knock my opponents off their trusty steads.

Take that quintain!

Let's get training

So, by now you can hold the lance, but can you control it? Jousting is all about precision and skill, so to test how well I could handle the lance ahead of my challenge, I was given a series of tasks to complete, which were all really good fun...

- **collect the crowns** Starting in walk, my task was to scoop my lance through the middle of some little crowns that were placed on the tilt. I picked this up quite quickly and was soon cantering down the line collecting them up easily
- **peasant's head** Using a spike attached to the end of the lance, I had to pick up a dummy's head from the ground while cantering past. I think I enjoyed this one a little bit too much!
- **slice the apple** Ok, so I didn't use my lance for this one but it was a tricky test of my control and hand-eye co-ordination. I had to canter past an apple on a pole and slice it cleanly in half with a sword. It took a few attempts, but eventually I got it and it was super-satisfying!

Take on the quintain

With my preliminary training complete, it was time to take on a mock joust with the quintain. The idea is to aim for the top right-hand corner of its shield for the perfect hit. There's a ball and chain attached to the opposite side, and the idea is that if you hit the shield in the wrong place, you get hit by it when the quintain spins! Thankfully I struck it in the right place, so I clearly have all the skills!

To the armoury

With my training complete, it was time to get kitted out in my full knight's attire! I had so much fun trying on all the different helmets – some of them were sooo heavy and like looking through a colander. Even Sausage had her own armour on and I'm not gonna lie, we definitely looked the part.

Time to joust

With my outfit on point, training complete and camera at the ready, it was time for my challenge against the Earl of Warwick. It was incredibly nerve-wracking cantering towards a knight who looked like he'd stepped straight out of the Middle Ages, but after a few goes I really got into it and even managed to break my lance on his shield. All my training paid off and I was awarded the title Warrior Princess!

Being a knight for the day is one of the most fun experiences I've ever had – if you love history, learning new horsey skills and cantering around one-handed, a jousting day is definitely for you.

Even my armour is matchy!

PERFECT *match*

Want to find out which of my horses you're most like?

I love all three of my horses equally, but they each have their own unique personalities, which makes them totally different. Take my fun quiz to find out whether you're most like Mickey, Casper or Joey!

1 **How would you describe yourself?**
 a) Clever and competitive
○ b) Cool and chilled
○ c) Chatty and funny

2 **Do you get nervous before a comp?**
○ a) Yes, really nervous! I worry about messing up
○ b) Nope – I've totally got this
☑ c) A little, but it helps me to feel even more excited!

3 **What's your favourite thing about going horse riding?**
○ a) Learning and training as much as I can
 b) Exploring new places on horseback
○ c) Having fun with friends

4 **What would you say you need to improve on the most?**
☑ a) Confidence – I need to learn to believe in myself
○ b) Motivation – sometimes I can be a little lazy when it comes to my work
○ c) Listening – I always have so much to say that I often talk too much!

5 **Which of these adventures sounds most fun to you?**
☑ a) Trying out a new cross-country course
 b) Going on an epic beach ride
○ c) Attending a pony party

6 **What role do you play in your friendship group?**
○ a) I'm good at thinking up fun things we can do together
 b) My friends always come to me when they need advice
○ c) I can make anyone laugh!

7 **What is your dream horsey job?**
☑ a) Pro rider – I would win lots of rosettes
○ b) Instructor – I could pass on my wisdom to others
○ c) Groom – I'd love pampering ponies all day long

8 **If you were a pony, what would be your fave activity?**
 a) Definitely jumping
○ b) Cantering across fields
○ c) Rolling around in mud

Mostly As Joey

You're most like Joey! As well as being cuddly and affectionate, he's super-athletic and enjoys any challenge. You're always up for learning new things and have talent to burn. However, Joey's young and can be unsure of situations he's not been in before – like him, you need to learn to believe in yourself and your abilities because you can do anything you put your mind to!

Mostly Bs Casper

If you were a horse you'd be just like Casper! Reliable and sure of himself, he is super-chill nowadays and doesn't take life too seriously. Your laid-back personality reminds me of his, but that doesn't mean you're not super-fun to be around, too! People are drawn to your positive energy. That's one of the things that makes you a great friend that people can always rely on.

Mostly Cs Mickey

Oh my goodness, you're just like Mickey! Aside from being totally adorable, Mickey definitely has a brilliant sense of humour as he can often be a little bit cheeky! Like him, you're the joker of your friendship group and are always making your mates laugh. You're probably a bit too chatty in the classroom, but you can't help it because you always have loads and loads to say!

a – 4
b – 3
c – 1

ANSWERS & TEMPLATES

Find all the answers and things you need here!

PAGE 14
WORDSEARCH

PAGE 15
SPOT THE DIFFERENCE

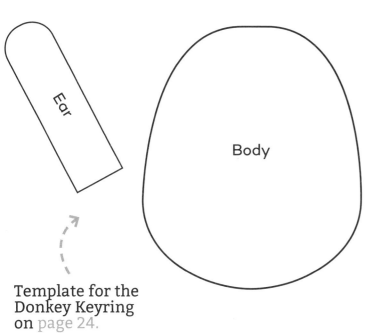

Ear

Body

Muzzle

Keyring loop piece

Template for the Donkey Keyring on page 24.

Sooo cute!

Love you x

Say cheese!

Template for the Painted rocks on page 36.